Heyer Guidance

IS
YOUR CHILD
DEPRESSED?

IS YOUR CHILD DEPRESSED?

Joel Herskowitz, M.D.

Pediatric Neurologist and Assistant Professor
at the Boston University School of Medicine

With the consultation of Charles W. Popper, Chief, Child and
Adolescent Psychopharmacology, Hall-Mercer Children's Center,
McLean Hospital, and Clinical Instructor in Psychiatry,
Harvard Medical School

PHAROS BOOKS
A SCRIPPS HOWARD COMPANY
NEW YORK

Cover design: Elyse Strongin

Text design: Nancy Eato

First published in 1988.

Library of Congress Cataloging-in-Publication Data
Herskowitz, Joel.
Is your child depressed?
Bibliography: p.
Includes index.
1. Depression in children—Popular works.   I. Title.
RJ506.D4H47   1988   618.92'8527   88-60372
Pharos ISBN 0-88687-356-8

Printed in the United States of America

Pharos Books
A Scripps Howard Company
200 Park Avenue
New York, NY 10166

10   9   8   7   6   5   4   3   2   1

To my children, Sylvan and Laurel

C O N T E N T S

You asked, "What's bothering you?" "Nothing," she said. "Then why don't you start smiling? All you ever do is mope!" She produced a few smiles the next few days. But her mood didn't change a bit.

Her schoolwork started to suffer. She didn't bring home assignments. Or she didn't do them. Those she turned in were sloppy and incomplete. She herself felt bad because she used to be a good student. But she couldn't seem to do anything about it.

Her sister overheard her muttering, "Everybody'd be happier if I were dead."

That caught your attention. It made you even more worried. Could she be depressed? Where were the sadness and tears? She wasn't sad. She wasn't tearful. She was irritable, continually out of sorts.

You brought her to your pediatrician for her annual checkup. He was too busy for anything other than a quick physical. No time to sit down and discuss your suspicion that something was wrong, really wrong.

Maybe it was your imagination, you thought. Maybe it was your fault. It was getting more confusing every day. You didn't know where to go for help.

Then, one day a magazine article caught your eye. Something about depressed children not being sad like adults, but "off" somehow in their behavior or emotional state. Angry, irritable, or just plain uninterested.

It began to ring true. When you got to the part about "sleeping all the time" and "no energy for anything," you knew what Jessica's problem was—depression.

For some reason, you immediately felt better. You grabbed the phone and made an appointment to see the pediatrician, this time by yourself.

"I know what's wrong with Jessica," you told the doctor. "She's depressed."

He listened to your story, glanced over the article you

CONTENTS

P R E F A C E

When I was twelve years old, I was browsing through the local library when I came upon a story in *Ripley's Believe It Or Not* that captivated me and has stayed with me for nearly three decades.

> A man with a long, dark cape entered the storefront office of a counselor and told a story of sadness. Filled with hopelessness and despair, he finished his tale and said: "I don't know if I can keep on going."
>
> "Ah," replied the wise man with enthusiasm, recognizing his caller's black mood, "I know just what you need. You must visit that incomparable clown, the great Grimaldi!"
>
> "But," the man responded, "you don't understand. I am Grimaldi."

That response washed over me like a wave of gloom. How ironic, how sad that the funny man himself suffered so profoundly. And nobody knew it!

If only someone could recognize what was going on and help him get better.

Reading this story, and reacting to it, was the birth of my awareness of depression—and how easily it can be overlooked.

I have since then had a keen interest in emotional problems. This interest and concern led to my formal training in child psychiatry after my pediatric residency, then to my becoming a neurologist who specializes in emotional and behavioral problems of children and adolescents.

As a pediatric neurologist, I see a large number of children with headaches. Naturally, parents are concerned about the possibility of brain tumor. So am I.

Over the past decade of practice, I have seen a significant pattern emerge. Among those hundreds of children with headaches, for every one who had a brain tumor, thirty were depressed.*

The depression was often unsuspected—by child, parents, or pediatrician. At other times, someone had suspected depression, but little or nothing was done about it. The child continued to suffer.

Childhood is supposed to be a time of exuberance and joy. What I was seeing was children whose lives were being drained of energy and enthusiasm.

I wanted to reach these depressed children somehow, to help them get the care they needed to get well. Writing exclusively for pediatricians and psychiatrists would be off the mark, I felt.

If I could reach parents of depressed children—parents who suspect that something is wrong but don't know how to give shape and direction to their observations and feelings— then these children could be helped to get better.

It is with these concerns and goals in mind that I have written this book.

I would like to thank the following people for their contributions: Dr. Ira Herskowitz, my twin brother, for his many valuable suggestions; Dr. Dennis Rosen and Ms. Patricia Rosen, for their helpful comments in reviewing the manuscript; Dr. Charles Popper, psychiatrist and psychopharmacologist, for his skilled consultation; and David Hendin, publisher, editor, author, and friend, who recognized the need for a book such as this one and provided great support through all stages of this project.

---

*One boy had a brain tumor *and* depression. Being depressed doesn't protect a person from having other problems as well!

Lastly, my deepest appreciation for the children and parents who allowed me to tell their stories so others will know that they're not alone and that with time and the right kind of help they will get better.

I would like to give special thanks to the child whose pictures of herself—depressed and well—speak so eloquently to the presence and character of depression in childhood and adolescence.

Joel Herskowitz, M.D.
Boston, Massachusetts

I N T R O D U C T I O N

Jessica's a crab. Not the kind that scuttles across the sand and terrorizes unsuspecting swimmers. She's your twelve-year-old daughter.

She wakes up on the wrong side of the bed every morning. When she comes to breakfast, everyone cringes. She's always miserable and makes everyone else miserable, too.

She's always yelling at her brother and sister. She used to have some friends, but not anymore. Not the way she acts. All she does is stay in her room, listen to the radio, or sleep.

Especially sleep. She can conk out in the middle of her favorite TV show. She takes a nap nearly every day after school, even though she doesn't take part in any sports.

When you suggest something to her, the usual reply is: "I don't have the energy."

You know something's wrong. But you're not sure what it is or what to do about it.

It started around eight months ago. You moved into your new home. There was nothing in particular to be unhappy about. She now had her own room. Her brother and sister had adjusted well to the move.

But Jessica was different. She kept getting worse: more miserable, more unhappy, more unpleasant for you and everyone else in the family to be around.

At first, you expected it to pass. It didn't. Then you actively encouraged her to get out and make new friends. She didn't have the energy. Children she did meet didn't ask her back.

You figured it was just laziness. So you got tough and pushed. Still no response. She became more miserable. You became angry and confused.

You asked, "What's bothering you?" "Nothing," she said. "Then why don't you start smiling? All you ever do is mope!" She produced a few smiles the next few days. But her mood didn't change a bit.

Her schoolwork started to suffer. She didn't bring home assignments. Or she didn't do them. Those she turned in were sloppy and incomplete. She herself felt bad because she used to be a good student. But she couldn't seem to do anything about it.

Her sister overheard her muttering, "Everybody'd be happier if I were dead."

That caught your attention. It made you even more worried. Could she be depressed? Where were the sadness and tears? She wasn't sad. She wasn't tearful. She was irritable, continually out of sorts.

You brought her to your pediatrician for her annual checkup. He was too busy for anything other than a quick physical. No time to sit down and discuss your suspicion that something was wrong, really wrong.

Maybe it was your imagination, you thought. Maybe it was your fault. It was getting more confusing every day. You didn't know where to go for help.

Then, one day a magazine article caught your eye. Something about depressed children not being sad like adults, but "off" somehow in their behavior or emotional state. Angry, irritable, or just plain uninterested.

It began to ring true. When you got to the part about "sleeping all the time" and "no energy for anything," you knew what Jessica's problem was—depression.

For some reason, you immediately felt better. You grabbed the phone and made an appointment to see the pediatrician, this time by yourself.

"I know what's wrong with Jessica," you told the doctor. "She's depressed."

He listened to your story, glanced over the article you

brought, and agreed. "I'd like you to meet a psychiatrist I know," he said. "She has a lot of experience with depressed children. I think Jessica will like her."

She did. And you liked how things turned out.

Jessica was angry at first. "Why do I have to go to a psychiatrist? I'm not crazy."

"I'm not saying you are," you replied. "But you are depressed. And a psychiatrist is a person who helps depressed children get better, to feel well again."

Jessica listened. Her angry mood was broken with tearful sobs. "I'm sick of feeling lousy!" she said.

With that, she agreed to meet the therapist you'd met and liked. The entire family met with her twice. Jessica continued weekly sessions for three months, then every other week for an additional month before her therapy was concluded.

Jessica enjoyed her visits with the psychiatrist. She felt the doctor really understood what she was feeling. She considered her psychiatrist to be someone, in addition to her parents, that she could turn to in a time of need.

So Jessica rejoined the human race. She was no longer a crab. Yes, she still had her moods. But they lasted hours, not weeks. And she herself could tell these were different from the depression that had dragged her down over the previous months.

She got along well enough with her brother and sister. Her schoolwork returned to its usual level. She went out with her friends on weekend bowling and movie dates.

Jessica had learned a lot about herself. And you learned a lot about yourself. You learned to trust your feelings. You felt something was wrong. And you were right.

You learned that if your other children developed symptoms of depression—or if Jessica's returned—you'd be quick to recognize it and get help without delay.

That was Jessica's story. It could just as well be the story of nine-year-old Richard, fifteen-year-old Leslie, or your child.

It is an all too common story. Gradual changes, barely noticed at first, occur over weeks to months. A worsening spiral of unhappiness, isolation, and misery. A spiral that can, and tragically sometimes does, lead to preventable death by suicide.

Depression *does* affect children and adolescents. It often looks very different from depression in adults. But that's not surprising because young people differ from grownups in so many ways.

At any age, depression hurts. It saps energy and joy from children at a time of life that's supposed to be creative and free.

Even sleep is not a sanctuary, for nightmares and difficulty in falling asleep can affect depressed children as often as extreme sleepiness.

They can gain an enormous amount of weight in a few months. Or become skinny without even trying. They no longer have the energy to do even the things they used to enjoy and be good at.

Their self-esteem plummets. Whose wouldn't if they didn't get along with anybody and there was nothing they really wanted to do! After a while, thoughts can turn to running away, or suicide.

Their families suffer, too. They suffer the unpleasantness of dealing with an irritable, unhappy child. They feel somehow responsible for causing the problem. They feel guilty for not getting help.

Is *your* child depressed? This book has been written to answer that question. If the answer is yes, it will help you get your child onto the road to well-being.

It will not make you a psychiatrist or psychologist. But it will provide you with useful tools toward establishing the diagnosis of depression.

With this knowledge plus your intuition, you can bring your focused concerns to a professional so your son or daughter can be treated and get better.

This book takes you step by step through the process of getting help for your child. It shows you how to put your own observations to use through a depression symptom checklist.

It tells you how to use this checklist so you can be referred to a child psychologist, psychiatrist, or other appropriate mental health professional. It tells you what to explain to your child before seeing a psychiatrist.

It presents the stories of depressed children and their families. You'll learn from others what depression is like in childhood and adolescence. You'll know your child is not alone.

You'll learn about the biological basis for depression. You'll learn about the role of your pediatrician and other specialists in the evaluation and treatment of your child.

You'll learn about suicide in childhood and adolescence and what simple preventive measures you can put into effect immediately.

You'll learn about the treatment of depression, including the possible role of medication.

Most of all, you will learn to have hope. Depression *can* be diagnosed. It *can* be treated. And *treatment helps.*

You're on a path designed to lead you to greater knowledge and more effective action. Let's now look further at what depression is and what it looks like in childhood.

Is Your Child Depressed? How You Can Tell

How do you know if your child is depressed?

There are fundamentally three ways. You ask. You observe. You seek.

You can ask directly: "Excuse me, David. Are you depressed?"

You may be startled by the answer you get: "Yes, I am. How can you tell?" "I have been ever since Grandpa died." "I was wondering how long it would take before someone noticed."

With that kind of acknowledgment, you can move ahead to make a plan for help.

What you may well encounter, though, is a negative response. Your daughter is depressed and not aware of it. Or denies it: "No. I'm feeling okay." "I was depressed last month, but I think I'm over it now." "I'm fine. Get off my back!"

☐

WHAT TO WATCH FOR

Regardless of the response you get, you must observe. What should you look for? *Mood* and *behavior*.

Let's say your sixteen-year-old daughter, who was previously an honor student, is failing two subjects. She's stopped going out with her friends and snaps at everyone in the family.

"Linda, I was wondering," you say at an opportune moment, "are you depressed?" "Leave me alone!" she responds, and runs off to her bedroom.

Where does that leave you? Observing her mood and behavior. Depression involves changes in both. After making further observations, guided by the helpful checklists in this chapter and the appendixes, you should seek professional help.

☐

EMOTION AND MOOD

To assist you in grasping the crucial concept of mood, I'd like to present a few simple definitions.

Mood is related to emotion. That's what you're feeling within yourself at a given moment. "I'm happy." "I'm sad." "I'm angry." "I'm tense." These are all everyday emotional states.

Your emotional state over a period of time—several days to several weeks—is your mood. It's the overall, sustained emotional state. It colors your every action and influences how you see and experience the world.

This emotional coloring is reflected in the popular use of the word "blue." "She's in a blue mood." "I don't know why he's been so blue lately." "He's singin' the blues." These common phrases are all examples of how mood casts its hue upon a person's life.

☐

EMOTIONAL CLIMATE

Another way to think of mood is as the "emotional climate." I don't mean the temperature from moment to moment, or the weather. Is it sunny or stormy? That's your current emotional state.

I'm speaking of the prevailing "climatic" condition. A cold front has been upon us now for over three weeks and shows no signs of letting up. A cloud of depression has been hanging over your head for several weeks, and it shows no signs of lifting.

The relationship between emotion and mood is summarized in this simple though powerful statement:

Emotion is to Mood
as
Weather is to Climate

This phrase* rolls off the tongue so smoothly, it's easy to miss its important message. Read it out loud slowly. Think of mood as the prevailing emotional climate. You'll then be better able to view the mood of your child—or yourself, for that matter.

□

TRYING TO BREAK THE SPELL

The mother of a depressed teenager told me: "His brother keeps trying to get Chuck to laugh. He seems to feel if he can only tell the right joke he'll break the spell [of depression]."

He might also be hoping that if he can get his brother to laugh, the depression's not that serious a problem.

Unfortunately, even if he does influence the local "weather" by making his brother chuckle, that won't do much, if anything, to change the overall emotional climate.

A sunny day in the Arctic or a cloudy day in the tropics doesn't alter the fundamental geography of the situation. (Mood, fortunately, is not anchored like a continent!)

□

APPEARANCES CAN MISLEAD

Appearances can be misleading when it comes to mood. A fourteen-year-old girl came to see me because of "headaches all the time."

---

*Adapted from *Diagnostic and Statistical Manual of Mental Disorders*. 3rd ed. Washington, D.C.: American Psychiatric Association, 1980.

"All the time" meant every waking hour for three months. That's a lot of headache. So I made sure she didn't have a brain tumor. I learned a great deal by listening to, and observing, her.

Her parents had been divorced for around a year. A classmate was killed in an automobile accident a month before the headaches began. Her grades worsened. Her friends dropped her.

She felt "totally miserable." But it wasn't obvious to most of those around her. "I'd smile on the outside," she said, "but not on the inside." What was inside, hidden from view, was sadness.

It wasn't fully hidden, however. Her face, as she told her story, was much less than fully animated. There was little if any crinkling at the corners of her eyes. Her lips did not move beyond the horizontal toward a smile. The folds between her upper lip and her nose lay flat. Her voice did not rise and fall normally in volume or melody.

Nor was her sadness deeply hidden. It was right below the surface—something that's typical of mood (be it happy or sad).

In this child and in others, the signs of depression are usually there—if you take the time to listen and observe.

□

DEPRESSION AS DISORDER

Before we go any further, I'd like to clarify a few things about the word "depression."

One of the confusing things about the term is that it means different things to different people at different times.

The mother of a depressed teenager noted ironically: "I went around all day saying 'I'm depressed.' It was a joke. I was bored and frustrated. It never occurred to me until later that my son was depressed!"

Getting out of the house cured her depression. His responded to psychotherapy.

□

NORMAL DEPRESSION

Depression is a normal part of life. It has been called a human being's response to loss, something everyone experiences from time to time. This response includes changes in emotional state and behavior.

Sometimes the word is used simply to mean sadness. In this book I use it to mean *depressive disorder*.

A child grieving for the death of his beloved dog is sad—not depressed—unless the sadness is extreme or prolonged. It would be extreme if, for example, associated with thoughts of suicide, prolonged if it interferes with his activities for weeks or months, not just a few days.

Thus, when sadness or other emotion *interferes significantly* with one or more areas of daily life, you have a disorder.

□

SPHERES OF ACTIVITY

I think of the child or adolescent functioning in several spheres of activity. These are (1) personal-social, (2) academic, (3) athletic, and (4) occupational.

The boy whose depression makes him withdrawn and irritable, a "drag" for his friends to be with, is not making it in the personal-social sphere.

The girl who got A's and B's first semester but C's and D's second semester because of her mood disturbance is impaired in the academic sphere.

The star athlete who loses interest in her favorite sport because of depression is compromised in the athletic sphere.

The boy whose sleepiness makes him late for work is experiencing difficulties in the occupational sphere.

Use the checklist in Table 1 to get a sense of the degree to which your child is participating in, or withdrawing from, different kinds of activities.

Table 1 ACTIVITY CHECKLIST

Has your son or daughter lost interest or pleasure in his or her usual activities over the past several weeks? Check those that apply.

	Not at All	Just a Little	Pretty Much	Very Much
Personal-Social	———	———	———	———
School	———	———	———	———
Sports	———	———	———	———
Job	———	———	———	———

□

POSITIVE AND NEGATIVE MOODS

As you observe your child's mood, a first step is to ask yourself: Is it positive or negative?

Positive moods are described by such words as happy, elated, friendly, cheerful, satisfied, good-tempered, agreeable.

Negative moods can be described as sad, angry, irritable, miserable, bad-tempered, spiteful, argumentative, resentful, hopeless, terrified, grouchy, ornery, annoyed, tense.

Use Table 2 to select the mood or moods that best describe your child. Then circle the number from one to ten in Table 3 that indicates how "up" or how "down" he or she is.

□

DEPRESSION WITHOUT SADNESS

A useful general term for these states of negative mood is *dysphoria*. A child or adolescent might simply call it "feeling bad."

When it comes to childhood depression, you don't have to have sadness or tears. You do generally have to have some form of dysphoria that lasts for two weeks or more.

Table 2   MOOD QUESTIONNAIRE

What has been your child's mood, his or her overall emotional state, over the past two weeks? Underline those choices that apply. Circle those few that apply best of all.

Sad	Blue	Tearful	Worried
Irritable	Fearful	Bored	Relaxed
Angry	Happy	Grouchy	Cheerful
Low	Withdrawn	Argumentative	Annoyed
Hopeless	Miserable	Discouraged	Tense
Down in the dumps	Nervous	Crabby	Bad-tempered

Table 3   MOOD SCALE

On a scale of 1 to 10, where 1 is very down (when a person has thoughts of committing suicide) and 10 is very up (when a person feels on top of the world), how would you rate your child's mood over the past two weeks? Circle one number.

DOWN   1   2   3   4   5   6   7   8   9   10   **UP**

☐

OBSERVING YOUR CHILD'S BEHAVIOR

Now that we've looked in detail at mood, let's turn to behavior. What is it about your child's behavior that will clue you in to the presence of depression?

Table 4 CHILDHOOD DEPRESSION CHECKLIST

Check the behavioral symptoms of depression that apply to your son or daughter. Bring this completed checklist and the others in this chapter to your physician or other professional for further discussion and planning.

Present   Absent

Present	Absent	
_____	_____	Marked loss of interest or pleasure in most, if not all, activities
_____	_____	Significant increase or decrease in appetite or weight (not due to dieting)
_____	_____	Sleep disturbance (too much sleep, difficulty falling asleep, nightmares)
_____	_____	Activity level increased or decreased (hyperactivity or sluggishness)
_____	_____	Fatigue or loss of energy nearly every day
_____	_____	Excessive or inappropriate guilt; low self-esteem
_____	_____	Problems in thinking in general or in concentrating; indecisiveness
_____	_____	Suicidal thoughts or actions
_____	_____	Physical complaints (headaches, stomach aches)

Adapted from "Diagnostic Criteria for Major Depressive Episode," *DSM-III-R*, American Psychiatric Association, 1987.

Table 5 PRESCHOOL DEPRESSION CHECKLIST

How does your preschool child behave with other children and adults? Fill in the blanks that describe your child's mood and behavior.

	Rarely or Never	Sometimes	Often	Always
Social Withdrawal				
Looks bored	____	____	____	____
Appears listless	____	____	____	____
Seems left out	____	____	____	____
Not interested in anything	____	____	____	____
Looks sad and tearful	____	____	____	____
Doesn't care about anything	____	____	____	____
Rejected by others	____	____	____	____
Avoids contact with others	____	____	____	____
Depression/Lack of Pleasure				
Not involved in activities	____	____	____	____
Not enthusiastic	____	____	____	____
Not having fun	____	____	____	____
Looks unhappy	____	____	____	____
Doesn't talk to other children	____	____	____	____
Cranky/Irritable				
Seems cranky or irritable	____	____	____	____
Needs to rest	____	____	____	____
Moody or changeable	____	____	____	____
Cries for no apparent reason	____	____	____	____

	Rarely or Never	Sometimes	Often	Always
Looks angry				
Seems tired				
Hyperactivity				
Constantly on the move				
Fidgety				
Hits or fights with others				
Talks a lot				
Rejects others				

Adapted from the General Rating of Affective Symptoms for Pre-schoolers (GRASP), developed by Helen Orvaschel, Ph.D. (See Kashani et al., 1986.)

The following paragraphs describe symptoms that identify children and adolescents with depression. As you read, fill in the Childhood Depression Checklist (Table 4). For preschool children (ages two to six), use the Preschool Depression Checklist (Table 5) as well.

The combination of behavior changes and disturbance in mood—such as sadness, irritability, or anger—strongly suggests a depressive disorder.

Bring the checklist to your doctor or other professional to discuss your concerns, confirm the presence of depression and move toward getting proper help for your child.

These descriptions of the symptoms of depression have been derived from current psychiatric diagnostic criteria and my medical practice.

1. **Loss of interest or pleasure.** The depressed child may show a marked loss of interest or pleasure in most, possibly all, of his or her usual pursuits.

Sometimes a person will use activities such as a job or sports to provide structure and keep himself going. Dropping out of basketball for no good reason or quitting an after-school art class can be signals of depression.

2. **Appetite or weight disturbance.** Because children and adolescents are growing beings, at times it can be difficult to know what is normal weight gain and what's excessive.

A gain (or loss) of 5 percent is a significant increase for an adolescent over a period of several weeks to a few months. For a teenager who weighs 150 pounds, this means a change of 7½ pounds. For younger children, growth charts are used to define a significant fall-off from anticipated gains.

Weight loss, particularly in adolescence, may raise the specter of anorexia nervosa. This is a serious eating disorder that often has a significant element of depression. Your pediatrician or other medical doctor can help you sort out this concern.

3. **Sleep disturbance.** Too much sleep, difficulty falling asleep, or frequent nightmares may occur in childhood depression.

Many teenagers normally have erratic sleeping habits. They burn the candle at both ends and "tank up"—get extra sleep—on weekends.

Getting home from school and falling asleep in midafternoon is not, however, normal in a physically well child. This sleepiness often has a drugged quality. In this situation, substance abuse (or overdosage of a prescribed medication) must be considered.

Difficulty getting to sleep may reflect not just depression but also anxiety. Lying down in quiet surroundings, the child or teenager does not have activities of the day to ward off troubling thoughts.

4. **Activity level.** Increased activity—the onset of fidgetiness or restlessness—can signify depression. It may also be a symptom of anxiety, which can coexist with a depressive disorder.

A significant slowdown in activity can also occur. The father of a fourteen-year-old depressed boy noted prolonged periods of "meditation" in his son at the onset of his mood disorder. "He'd just sit there doing nothing."

5. **Fatigue or loss of energy.** "I don't have the energy" could be the theme for many depressed children and adolescents.

You may not be readily able to appreciate a mood disturbance. But the overwhelming lack of "get up and go"—unresponsive to parental encouragement, support, or threats—should provide a major clue to depression.

Once again, it is essential that a comprehensive medical evaluation be carried out to ensure that a physical disorder is not causing or contributing to a marked behavioral change.

Remember, teenagers in particular are often reluctant or unwilling to share their feelings of sadness with parents. So you must observe your child's behavior and activity (the "bottom line" of mood), understand what you're seeing, and act on that information.

6. **Guilt or low self-esteem.** Depressed children may feel guilty for no reason at all, or their guilt may be exaggerated. This seems to be more characteristic of adult depression, but it occurs in childhood and adolescence as well.

Feeling bad about oneself can interfere significantly with peer, sibling, and family interactions. Once things get into a negative groove, it's tough for the child to get back on track and avoid a depressive spiral.

7. **Thinking or concentration problems.** Once again, a *change* in behavior is what you're looking for. Your child previously focused well in school, finished assignments on time, completed homework on schedule. Now, assignments are incomplete, sloppy, or lost.

Difficulty concentrating is characteristic, too, of children with anxiety or attentional disorders. Either or both of these can coexist with a depressive disorder.

Problems with thinking may be manifested by difficulty in making decisions.

8. **Suicidal thoughts or actions.** There's a tremendous spectrum of self-harm. It ranges from statements spoken in momentary frustration—"I wish I was dead!"—to more action-oriented exclamations—"I'm going to kill myself." Suicidal behavior that may occur with little or no apparent warning.

The subject of suicide is covered in detail in Chapter 8. A suicidal statement by a child must always be taken seriously.

9. **Physical complaints.** Headaches, stomach aches, even the proverbial pain in the neck may be important indicators of depression.

Not only medical examination but often subspecialty evaluation may be necessary to exclude physical illness such as brain tumor, stomach ulcer, or arthritis. You as parent should keep the possibility of depression in mind and bring it to the attention of the doctors evaluating your child.

With the checklists in this book and your knowledge of your child, it should be possible for the diagnosis of depression to be made by inclusion rather than merely exclusion.

It's always possible to do one more test. A so-called psychiatric diagnosis such as depression should not be established only when the doctors have run out of tests to do.

You may well spare your child painful, time-consuming, and expensive testing. And, of course, you'll be on track toward helping your child get better!

☐

WHEN TO BE SUSPICIOUS OF DEPRESSION

Some situations are setups for depression:

• Separation or divorce of parents, or even of close relatives
• The death of a loved one—person or pet

- A move from one town, or even one neighborhood, to another

- Academic failure (which is often an effect of depression but may be a cause)

- A physical illness (be it a broken leg or diabetes) requiring hospitalization or curtailment of activity.

A common denominator of these situations is *change*, and, more specifically, *loss*.

Sometimes the loss arises out of a positive situation. Take, for example, the adolescent going off to college. This involves many changes, many losses—customary surroundings, family of origin, often a boyfriend or girlfriend left behind or attending another school.

Sometimes depression arises from loss of face. The child who, on a lark, steals something she could easily have paid for and gets caught may experience embarrassment and shame immediately. Depression—even to the point of suicide—may follow.

The perfectionistic child may suffer intense depression from a self-perceived failure to live up to academic or athletic standards that many would consider too high.

Sometimes there is no apparent loss. This can happen under conditions of secrecy, as with sexual abuse, when the pain is hidden deeply inside because of extreme threat.

Depression can happen for no identifiable reason whatsoever, as if a switch is thrown and depression turned on.

□

ACKNOWLEDGING YOUR
CHILD'S FEELINGS

Being suspicious of depression doesn't mean you should go on a witch hunt determined to find something even if it isn't there.

If you do recognize some elements of depression, it would be appropriate for you to acknowledge how your child is feeling. For example, after a family move: "Chris, I can tell how hard it is for you to make a whole new set of friends."

That kind of comment opens the door for communication. In that way, disturbing feelings are not bottled up inside. The path to further discussion is cleared.

If you have doubts as to whether the adjustment process is proceeding in a normal manner, seek professional help.

□

ASSOCIATED PROBLEMS

Depression—a major depressive disorder—may not exist in pure form. It may occur along with one or more other problems. These include (1) manic-depressive (bipolar) disorder, (2) anxiety disorder, (3) attentional disorders, and (4) learning disabilities such as dyslexia. More detailed diagnostic criteria are included in the appendixes.

In some children, the periods of depression—"down" phases—are mixed with manic periods—"up" phases. In many respects, manic periods are the flip side to depressive episodes.

The mood is typically elevated though it may be irritable as with depression. Behavioral changes include diminished need for sleep, tremendously increased energy, talkativeness, grandiose schemes fueled by overconfidence.

Family history may provide a clue to this *manic-depressive, or bipolar, disorder*. A parent, uncle, or grandparent may have experienced the same problem and may have been successfully treated with lithium.

Anxiety disorders often coexist with depression. The hallmark of this group of disorders is anxiety—what has been called the body's anticipation of loss.

Anxiety is manifested by apprehensive expectation. Associated symptoms include muscle tension, restlessness, shortness of breath, rapid heart rate, dry mouth, "butterflies in the stomach," frequent urination, hyperalertness.

Attentional disorders are marked by easy distractibility and impulsivity. Hyperactivity need not be part of the picture.

For children with attentional problems and learning disabilities, school can be a thoroughly discouraging—indeed, truly depressing—experience.

☐

JIMMY

I saw Jimmy, a ten-year-old fifth-grader, in consultation because, as he described it, "I fight a lot."

Early in elementary school, he was recognized as having attentional problems. He did best in a one-to-one situation or sitting close to the teacher so she could guide him back to his work.

Socially, he had more significant difficulties. "He craves friends," his mother said. "But he doesn't know how to keep them." He tended to be bossy and got into a lot of fights on the playground.

I found Jimmy to be a fidgety boy with a normal neurologic examination. He did not seem depressed or anxious.

Jimmy told me how frustrating it was for him not to have any friends. I reviewed symptoms of depression with him and learned of his dwindling self-esteem and sleep disturbance. Jimmy had a recurring nightmare in which his head was chopped off.

COMMENT. Jimmy had an attention deficit disorder with hyperactivity. He also had a mood problem, manifested not by sadness but by irritability and anger. In addition, he had a sleep disturbance in the form of nightmares.

Most of the time, people wake up or otherwise manage to avoid death or injury in their scary dreams. It has been said that being killed or sustaining physical harm in the dream indicates depression.

Jimmy's attentional disorder made it hard for him to maintain positive interactions with peers. So, despite his best efforts to make friends, he had frustrating, unrewarding experiences.

The school seemed to be doing a good job of helping Jimmy compensate for his distractibility. The major ongoing problem was getting along with peers.

I suggested his parents arrange for psychiatric consultation to look into the degree to which depression was interfering with Jimmy's life. His school enrolled him in weekly sessions with other children who had behavior problems.

A *learning disability* is defined by a gap (usually two years) between intellectual level and level of academic achievement. A learning disability in the area of reading is termed *dyslexia*. This problem often runs in families in much the same way that positive attributes, such as musical ability, tend to.

As a general rule, I suspect attentional disorder in any child I encounter with a learning disability. When hyperactivity is not present, attentional disorders are extremely easy to overlook.

The combination of the two—learning disability and attentional disorder—can be doubly stressful, doubly depressing for a child.

□

PROFESSIONAL HELP

The last part of the process is for you to seek professional help. You've asked. You've observed. You've filled out the checklists in this chapter.

Now, it's time to bring this information to a professional. Your child's pediatrician is well suited to carry things forward. If depression is severe and suicide is an active concern, you might contact a psychiatrist, psychologist, social worker, or other mental health professional.

Rabbis, ministers, and priests can also play an important role in confirming your suspicions, providing support, and getting you further along on the road to health for your child.

Now that you have a better idea of how depression appears in childhood and adolescence, let's look at three case studies and learn how depression affected these children and their families.

2

Getting Well: The Story of Three Children

Children being children, they're not likely to announce to their parents, "I'm depressed. Please get me to a psychiatrist."

A more likely scenario is that the child suffers for weeks and months while everyone else in the family suffers along with them. Then, finally, the mother or father, when she or he can no longer stand the irritability, tries to do something about it.

Very often what comes next is a parade of doctors who toss around a variety of diagnoses and rule out nasty conditions like brain tumors. Sometimes this is productive. At other times, not.

It can leave the family confused—and the child still depressed. Finally someone takes the bull by the horns, and the problem is definitively identified. It's explained to the child and family. A treatment plan for the depression is made and put into effect.

In this chapter, I present the stories of three children with depression as they unfolded over several years. Their names and other identifying information, as in later chapters, have been withheld or slightly modified in order to maintain confidentiality.

Reading these stories, you will get more of a feel for different ways that depression can appear in childhood and adolescence. It usually enters in a sneaky, insidious way. At some point, however, it becomes clear there has been a change—a persisting change—in the child's behavior and emotional state.

These are not fairy-tale "happily ever after" situations that you encounter in books. Just as it often takes a while for the depression problem to be recognized, it takes a while for it to be resolved.

Understanding helps. Patience helps. Therapy helps. All these factors can work together as you seek to restore the well-being of your child, your family, and yourself.

☐

MICHAEL

When Michael was thirteen years old, he was struck by a car while riding his bike to the store on an errand. He didn't break any bones and wasn't knocked out. But he was certainly shaken up. The doctor who examined him in the emergency room felt he had suffered a mild concussion.

Over the next few weeks, his parents noted a change in Michael's behavior. "He was an outstanding athlete, highly motivated," his mother recalled. "After the accident, he started missing practice. The coach talked to him, but it didn't make any difference."

He had been a pretty good student. "He worked hard, but managed to get mostly B's," his mother said. His grades fell to the C and D range.

She described a change in his sleep, too. "He went to bed around 11, but didn't fall asleep until 2 A.M." He was grumpy in the morning and throughout the day. "He got into fights with his brother and sister for no reason at all," his father noted.

He had stomach aches nearly every day. His pediatrician checked him and found him normal. Because of daily headaches, he was referred to me for further evaluation.

When I examined Michael, I found him to be a healthy-appearing teenager. He did not look anxious or depressed. His neurologic examination was entirely normal. Because of the frequent headaches, mood disturbance, and head trauma, I ordered a CAT scan of his head.

It was normal. In the next month, the rest of Michael headed in that direction, too. He slept better. His grades improved. He was less irritable. His headaches and stomach pains disappeared entirely.

Things continued to go well until the fall, when he returned to school. Headaches, stomach pains, and irritability recurred with full force. "I couldn't tell if he was grouchy because of the pain or because something was bothering him," his mother said.

His pediatrician again cleared him from the medical standpoint.

I found Michael to be mildly anxious. When I asked him what was bothering him, he told me, "Ninth grade's a lot tougher than eighth." He was finding it difficult to keep up with his schoolwork.

His mother confirmed this academic stress. There didn't seem to be anything else going on in his life that could account for his change in mood and behavior.

He underwent educational and psychological testing in school. His schedule was adjusted, and things went smoothly for the rest of the school year.

A year and a half later, Michael's mother called me. "He hasn't slept for the past week—maybe one hour a night. And his attitude is rotten," she said. "Nobody in the family can stand him!"

At my office, I spoke with Michael while his parents were out of the room. Yes, he had slept little over the past few weeks, as little as half an hour per night. He was less animated than usual. His usual sparkle was gone. I didn't know if it was simply fatigue or part of a mood disturbance.

"How have you been feeling lately?" I asked. "Hassled," he said. He considered himself usually mild-mannered. "Now when someone bothers me, I feel like punching 'em out," he said. And he had been crying a lot.

"Sometimes when people are down," I said, "they think of hurting themselves. Maybe even committing suicide. Have you had any thoughts like that?"

"No," he replied. "I have thought of running away, though. I've got to get outta there!"

I learned from Michael's mother that she and her husband

had been separated for five months. It looked as if they were heading for divorce. Michael was taking it all very hard.

His parents were involved in counseling. But I felt that Michael was so depressed it was essential for him to be seen as soon as possible by a psychiatrist or psychologist.

I told Michael's mother I didn't consider him to be at high risk for suicide at that time. But I asked that his father's hunting rifle be removed from the home and that all unnecessary medications be thrown out.

Michael met weekly with a child psychiatrist for three months in individual therapy and had several sessions involving his entire family. Marital counseling continued throughout.

"Having someone to talk to outside the family was extremely helpful," his mother said. "Michael was very caught up in the whole separation process. He felt he had to take sides, and it was tearing him up.

"His therapist has helped him to make decisions for himself and lead his own life," she said.

Eight months after I first saw him, Michael was in good spirits, getting on with his life on all fronts. He wound up repeating the school year but was doing well academically. He had a part-time job on weekends and was looking forward to basketball season.

COMMENT. Michael's story has taken us through several episodes of relatively minor depression and one that was quite severe.

Three different situations brought out his depression. The first episode was triggered by an accident that shook him up emotionally as well as physically.

An automobile accident, even a near miss, can be very scary for children, whether they're the bicyclist, passenger, or pedestrian.

The child's reaction to nearly being killed is intensified by his parent's response. They're likely to feel guilty because of their real or imagined role in the accident. In their efforts to make sure another mishap doesn't occur, they may come down hard on the child.

A clue to the second episode was the time it occurred. School had just gotten back in session. Michael was dismayed to find his previous skills were not enough to meet the new academic demands.

The third episode was brought about by his parents' marital separation and threatened divorce. The losses here are obvious: among the most important, the loss of the intact family and one parent or the other. The uncertainties of separation and divorce can generate a great deal of anxiety. That can interfere with a child's life as much as depression.

During the first two periods of depression, I didn't feel that psychiatric referral was necessary. I stayed in touch with the family, though, and would have made such a referral if things had not gotten better.

The third episode, by contrast, was much more intense. Psychiatric referral was clearly necessary. Michael and his parents had no difficulty accepting that recommendation.

Different kinds of counseling—individual, family, and marital—were pursued by Michael and his family. All three contributed to his getting better and doubtlessly added to the well-being of other family members, too.

Children tend to feel events around them result magically from their thoughts and actions. Therapy can help them get a more realistic sense of their role and responsibility.

□

VICKY

Fifteen-year-old Vicky was having a difficult summer. "Everything was blurry," she recalled. What was even more odd:

"I went on a camping trip and it felt like I was there and not there."

She got back to school and things were still not right: "I felt dazed, spacey—like I was in a dream." Her schoolwork didn't suffer. But she didn't feel much like going out with her friends, and they stopped calling her.

Instead of being cheerful, upbeat, and energetic, her mother found her "obnoxious, fresh, and rude." Vicky was "aggravated" easily and was always tired. "Even twelve hours of sleep weren't enough," her mother said.

"She slept constantly," her father recalled. "We thought of drugs. But, except for one incident with alcohol, it wasn't a factor."

Vicky's mother brought her to the pediatrician. She was checked for infectious mononucleosis ("mono"), sinusitis, and urinary infection. All negative. She saw an eye specialist for the blurry vision. He didn't find anything either.

"I knew something was wrong," Vicky's mother recalled. "But I wasn't able to put my finger on it. She said she didn't feel well but couldn't say just what was bothering her.

"Finally I asked her outright: 'Are you depressed?' She said no."

Vicky was nonetheless evaluated by a psychologist. She found evidence for tension headaches and mild depression. Relaxation exercises were suggested and additional testing recommended in several months.

Meanwhile, things got worse. Headaches became more severe. Her mother was not satisfied with the evaluations. And Vicky was brought to see me for consultation.

When I first met Vicky, her facial expression was tense. She sat stiffly in her chair, showing mild anxiety. She appeared a bit sad, too. She didn't feel particularly anxious or sad but still had the "blurry," unreal feeling. Her neurologic examination was entirely normal.

Looking at Vicky's excessive sleeping, social withdrawal,

and altered emotional state, I felt she had a mood disorder. It was not typical depression. But it was close enough that that's what I called it.

"That was the happiest day in my life," Vicky's mother told me recently, three years later. "When you said to me 'I know what's wrong with your child' and you were going to help her get well."

Simply knowing that this mysterious, disabling, and troubling condition had a name—depression—proved to be helpful for the entire family!

Vicky's father added: "Parents should know that depression is treatable, curable. Not to treat it—just looking the other way—can be fatal."

The first order of business was to get Vicky teamed up with a therapist. Things didn't work out well at the beginning. "I didn't like my first psychiatrist," Vicky recalled. "I don't know why. He just made me feel bad."

But her parents, with my encouragement, insisted she see someone else. They made it abundantly clear that therapy was not optional.

Vicky did, however, have a say in the matter. "My mother told me: 'If you don't like this therapist, we'll find someone else.' "

What did Vicky think about the second psychiatrist? "The first few times, he was just another doctor," she recalled. "He sat in a big overstuffed chair with his legs crossed. He didn't say a whole lot usually. But he listened, and he'd add some really eye-opening insights. The talks helped a lot."

Vicky would have liked things to improve more rapidly. "I was hoping to wake up one morning and be 100 percent well," she said. It was, however, a more gradual process. Within five months she was back to normal.

Through her own experience she became so tuned in to depression that she recognized it in one of her friends and guided her to therapy.

"Her parents just felt she had an attitude problem. But I knew exactly what she was going through," she said. "And it was not getting better by itself."

COMMENT. The road to well-being for Vicky was neither clear nor straight. (It certainly wasn't short, either!) Her physical difficulties led to medical evaluation, which pointed toward depression. But the seriousness of the problem was not recognized and a suitable plan was not made.

At first, Vicky's father was skeptical about all the doctors' visits—and about the diagnosis of depression: "What was there for her to be depressed about?"

Indeed, there was no particular circumstance or stress that was ever identified. It just more or less happened.

Vicky's father knew from his own adolescence that it was a time of ups and downs. He became increasingly aware over time that something was wrong with his daughter, more than just a passing phase.

What was the key here? I'd like to think it was my involvement. It really wasn't. The person most responsible for Vicky's getting better, for getting her the help she needed, was her mother.

"Her availability, willingness to listen, and persistence made all the difference," said Vicky's father. Her sense that things were not right and her refusal to quit until she got answers to her questions paved the way for her daughter's return to health.

□

ROBERT

I first met Robert four years ago. He was an overweight, angry, and uncommunicative sixteen-year-old. Today, he's a trim, cheerful, and thoughtfully articulate young adult.

What happened? How did he get depressed? How did he get better? I met recently with Robert and his parents. They told me what it was like for them during his depression and what helped.

Robert wasn't always heavy. During the six months before I saw him, he'd gained 50 pounds. He weighed 235 pounds at a height of five feet eight inches. "He couldn't seem to fill himself up," his mother recalled.

Nor could he seem to get enough sleep. He slept twelve to fifteen hours a night and still woke up tired.

He had been an honor student. But his concentration was "shot," as he termed it; and he was in danger of repeating the year with a string of F's.

His parents knew that things were not right because of his mood. "He was angry all the time!" his mother said.

The sleeping problem finally prompted his mother to bring Robert to the pediatrician. "It just wasn't normal to sleep that much. Especially since he wasn't going out for sports," his mother recalled.

His pediatrician recognized the changes in mood and behavior, and referred Robert to a psychiatrist. Because of the persistent headaches, he also sent him to me for evaluation.

At our first meeting, Robert told me, "I've had this tiredness, dizziness, and pressure in my head for two years."

He had no evidence for a brain tumor as I checked his reflexes and looked inside his eyes for evidence of swelling. I did a CAT scan anyway, because brain tumors can cause exactly what Robert suffered from: headaches and mood disturbance.

I saw him a few weeks later to tell him the test results and find out how he was doing. He was more at ease as we spoke, and it became additionally clear he was suffering from depression. Except that he didn't feel depressed!

At least he didn't feel sad. Nor did he look sad. "Well, Robert," I asked, "how *do* you feel?"

He thought for a moment and said, "Nervous. Like when you get into a basketball game for the first time. Only the feeling doesn't go away."

What was even more upsetting to him was that three or four times a week for the past six months he'd been having episodes of outright panic. They came out of the blue and lasted around a minute. "My heart beat like crazy and I felt like I was going to lose my mind," he said. He trembled, perspired profusely, and had to sit down because he felt so shaky.

I was momentarily stunned. Not only had Robert been experiencing serious depression, but he'd also had these terrifying panic attacks to deal with. People had guessed at the depression, but the panic episodes had been kept secret.

"Robert," I asked, "why didn't you tell anyone about those episodes?" He replied: "Nobody asked."

Because the depression and the anxiety were so upsetting and disabling, I started him on a medication (imipramine) known to be effective with both problems.

Almost immediately, the free-floating anxiety and panic attacks disappeared. Said Robert at the time: "Now I don't get nervous for no reason."

The depression took longer to come around. Over the course of several months, during which he received supportive therapy, his depression improved. He noted wryly that "even the dog became more tolerable. I used to hate it."

He got back on the honor roll and was graduated with honors. He entered a technical school the next fall on a scholarship. His sleep returned to normal, eight or nine hours nightly. Looking back, Robert recalled: "Before, I was tired all the time. I couldn't control it. Now when I'm tired, there's a reason for it."

During the first few months of his depression, Robert didn't realize what was going on—"It's tough to say you're depressed if you don't know anything different." And it took place gradually, which made it difficult for him or his parents to notice the change.

"It's like a slide. You don't know it's happening. You tell yourself: 'That's just me. And that's just how it's got to be.' At the bottom, you kill yourself, or you start climbing out of it."

Once he started feeling better, which took several months, exercise became an important part of his routine. "It clears your head," he said. "It's a chemical thing. Something to do with dopamine."

Robert had taken special interest in his psychology course. He brought in his textbook to show me. The sections on depression and anxiety were heavily underlined.

His weight returned to normal, too. At last count, he'd lost fifty-five pounds—without suffering.

COMMENT. There are many important lessons to be learned (and relearned) from Robert's story.

The mood component of his depression was not sadness. His overall emotional state was anger as perceived by his parents, nervousness as he felt it.

He did not have just one problem—depression. He had a second—anxiety—which occurred both as generalized nervousness and as discrete panic attacks.

In fact, depression and anxiety often occur together, in the same person and within families. In Robert's family, no one had major depression. But an aunt had an anxiety disorder.

Having a relative with major depression or an anxiety disorder appears to stack the deck biochemically. In other words, it seems to make it more likely that, under the right (or wrong) set of circumstances, the child, adolescent, or adult will experience a mood disorder.

In Robert's case, there was no single event that triggered his depression. It appeared to be a combination of his adapting to adolescence and, perhaps, difficulties dealing with his siblings.

During the months I met with Robert, his mother spoke regularly with her priest, which she felt was very helpful. She also took part in a support group in her community for parents of troubled (and troubling) teenagers.

Now that you've had a chance to meet these children and their families, let's look at what *you* should do if you think your child is depressed.

3

What to Do If You Think Your Child Is Depressed

A t this point in the book, your hunches about depression may be ready for dismissal. On the other hand, maybe your suspicions are being confirmed. Your daughter really does seem to be depressed.

On the Activity Checklist, you've recorded her loss of interest in school and sports. You've selected "irritable" and "argumentative" as the moods that best fit. Her emotional state over the past two weeks has been a 4, definitely on the down side.

You've filled out the Depression Checklist, and it's there in black and white: sleep disturbance, hyperactivity, fatigue, and frequent stomach aches.

You can't blink it away. You can't chalk it up to adolescent moodiness. It does look like depression.

Now what do you do? You need professional help from both medical and mental health professionals. The purpose of this chapter is to take you through the next step in getting help for your child: medical evaluation.

□

NEED FOR MEDICAL AND MENTAL HEALTH SPECIALISTS

This chapter will tell you, your spouse, and your child what to expect. That should help to minimize confusion, misunderstanding, and anxiety. It should facilitate confirmation of the diagnosis of depression so your child can get better as soon as possible.

You will need to see a medical specialist—a pediatrician, family practitioner, or other appropriate physician. You will also need to see a specialist in the mental health field—a psychiatrist, psychologist, social worker, or other qualified professional.

In this way, you can be confident that you'll touch all the bases, paying proper attention to the *whole* child.

The first thing to do is to make an appointment for a general physical examination, a medical checkup. Keep in mind, this is not a slap-the-stethoscope-on-the-chest, quickie physical for camp.

What you need is a thoughtful exploration of physical factors—from brain tumor to ulcerative colitis—that might cause your child's tiredness, headaches, irritability, weight loss, or other symptoms you've observed.

An exception to this order of business is if you feel your child is suicidal. In that case, call your doctor immediately. Express clearly your concerns about suicide. Make arrangements then and there for psychiatric consultation.

Now for the pediatrician.

Making an Appointment

The first step is to pick up the telephone and call your physician. You're likely to get a secretary or nurse. Be prepared. Know why you're calling and what you're aiming to set up.

That way you won't be put off by the receptionist saying, "But Mrs. Harris, Jimmy just had his yearly physical." Try this instead:

Mrs. Harris: "I'm worried about Jimmy. He's sleeping too much. And he's slipped from the honor roll for the first time in years. I think he might be depressed. Before I see a psychologist, I want Dr. Johnson to check him over and make sure it's not a physical illness."

Secretary: "I understand what you're saying, Mrs. Harris. Why don't you bring him in to see Dr. Johnson this Wednesday."

Mrs. Harris: "Will Jimmy and I have a chance to speak with Dr. Johnson separately? I think it would be important. He's older now, and there may be things he has difficulty telling me that he'd tell the doctor."

Secretary: "That's a good point. I'll schedule him for half an hour at the end of the day instead of the usual fifteen-minute time slot for physicals."

Preparation for the Visit

Preparing your child for the examination is a good idea: "I've made an appointment for you to see Dr. Johnson. You just haven't seemed well lately. And I wanted you to have a checkup."

Younger children will invariably respond: "Will I get any shots?"

Since you're unable to read the future, the best thing to say is "I don't know." Or "We'll see. The doctor will decide if any tests are necessary. He might be able to figure out what's causing your headaches and sluggish feelings by checking your blood."

Saying no to avoid a tearful scene would be tantamount to lying or tricking your child. That could put your doctor—and you—in an awkward position at a time when trust is particularly important.

Prepare yourself for the visit, too. Make sure you've filled out the checklists in Chapter 1. Don't leave this book at home. Bring it with you to the doctor's office.

Think about the events and episodes that might have caused or contributed to your child's change in behavior and mood. A marital separation, an impending move, the death of a beloved pet would be significant for any member of the family.

Even things that might seem good, like making the soccer team or getting a girlfriend, might be complicated and stressful. The pressures in a child's life can have an extremely powerful effect, especially when they're not talked about.

At the Doctor's Office

You've done your homework. So your visit should be a valuable one. Remember your goals: (1) to determine if there are medical causes for your child's problems and (2) to prepare the way for psychiatric or psychologic referral, if that's where things are heading.

Make sure you allow your child to speak on his or her behalf. That means through body language as well as verbal language. Don't, in your own anxiety, admonish your daughter to "Sit up straight" or "Look at the doctor."

The "slouch sign" can be a valuable clue that there's an emotional problem. "When we first meet," said a specialist in adolescence I work with, "many kids are a bit shy and look away. But when I'm practically down on the floor trying to establish eye contact, I know something's up."

That "something" is likely to be an emotional problem.

Let your child speak for himself. When the doctor asks, "What brings you here today, Jimmy?" he may get a facetious reply ("The bus"). A grunt. Or, what may shock you, a lucid, articulate reply: "I haven't had the energy for anything lately. I think I'm depressed."

Speaking Alone with the Doctor

Your teenager (or even a younger child) may not talk when you're in the room. So if the doctor doesn't suggest it, offer to leave.

You, too, should have the opportunity to speak with the physician alone. This will give you the chance to touch upon things you're concerned about that may be relevant to your child's mood and behavioral disturbance.

There are many topics—suicidal feelings in a parent, a threatened marital separation, suspected sexual abuse—

that are not appropriate for the child to overhear. Learning of such issues from a parent, the doctor can then—in conversation with the child alone—be alert to them or bring them out for discussion.

Be sure you make clear that you're concerned about the possibility of depression. If your suspicions, supported by the materials you've brought, are borne out, you may wish to pursue psychiatric or psychologic evaluation.

The physician should, of course, understand that you're there for your child to undergo careful examination and any tests (such as thyroid hormone measurement or drug screening) that seem appropriate to the problems at hand.

☐

MEDICAL CAUSES OF DEPRESSION

The doctor's evaluation will consist of three parts: history, examination, and investigation.

The history is essentially an interview. Let's assume you've brought your son to the doctor. She starts by asking why he's there.

Resist the temptation to blurt out what's been churning inside you recently: "Doctor, I think he's depressed!" It's important that your child respond directly to the doctor. It may well be that what's bugging him is "My head's killing me!" or "I haven't been able to sleep for the last week."

If the doctor knows where your son is coming from—what the child is experiencing—she can communicate directly with him. That's crucially important when you're dealing with depression and other emotional disorders.

The doctor will ask when a symptom was first noticed and what's been done about it. With depression, there may be several symptoms to track down—headache, fatigue, irritability. So the interview period can take more than a couple of minutes.

It's useful for you to know what's going on in the mind of the physician during this part of the medical process. She may well have been convinced in your brief telephone conversation that the problem is depression.

The Doctor's Inner Dialogue

What's going on now is a conversation inside the doctor's head. It might go something like this:

"Yes, I think it *is* depression."

"But that's not the only thing that can cause fatigue, belly pain, and irritability."

"Well then, how about a gastrointestinal problem—colitis or an ulcer?"

This kind of self-talking prompts further questioning along specific medical avenues. "Have you noticed a change in your bowel habits?" "Have you been sick to your stomach lately?" "Do you feel that any foods disagree with you?"

□

CATEGORIES OF ILLNESS

When depression is the primary concern, several categories of medical illness should be considered. These include (1) medical, (2) neurologic, and (3) toxic.

I won't attempt a comprehensive list of every condition that can cause or masquerade as depression. That's beyond the scope, and not the purpose, of this book. But I would like to present a few conditions I feel are particularly important.

□

MEDICAL CONDITIONS

Just about any medical disorder can contribute to fatigue, weight loss, irritability, change in sleeping patterns, or withdrawal from usual activities. Any or all can suggest depression.

To complicate matters further, teenagers can drag themselves out by pushing themselves too hard academically, socially, or athletically—"burning the candle at both ends."

A child whose weight loss and fatigue have been associated with diarrhea may have a gastrointestinal disorder such as colitis or ileitis.

When fatigue and weight loss are combined with muscle weakness and skin rash, an inflammatory disorder of muscle—dermatomyositis—should be considered. it has been said that "weakness plus misery equals dermatomyositis."

Diabetes in Childhood

Diabetes (that is, diabetes mellitus, or "sugar diabetes") can mimic depression, too. Children of any age—infancy through adolescence—can insidiously develop fatigue, weight loss, and irritability as they lose tremendous amounts of water and sugar through their urine. This happens because they lack insulin, the chemical that facilitates entry of glucose into cells where it can be used as fuel.

Once diabetes has been diagnosed, emotional issues nearly always come to the fore. There's anxiety about handling the needles, giving injections, taking too much insulin.

Depression, too, typically enters the picture. The child and family may struggle in coming to grips with a lifelong, often life-shortening illness, potentially complicated by kidney failure and blindness, that requires attention seven days a week.

Thyroid and Calcium Problems

Another disorder of metabolism that can look like depression is hypothyroidism, underactivity of the thyroid gland.

Situated within the front of the neck, the thyroid gland works closely with the brain to make sure activity and metabolism are not too speeded up or slowed down.

Children with hypothyroidism actually tend to be very well behaved. It's when they're treated (with thyroid hormone) that they can disturb others as they achieve a normal level of rambunctiousness.

Before that time, though, they may be the picture of depression, or at least some aspects of it. They tend to move slowly, gain weight easily, and sleep more than usual.

An excess of calcium in the blood (hypercalcemia) can also slow things down and look like depression, or even make a person depressed. Calcium is virtually everywhere in the body and brain. Too much calcium slows the heart, quiets the deep tendon reflexes, and depresses the mood.

There are many causes for hypercalcemia. One of them is a tumor of the parathyroid glands. Situated in the neck near the thyroid, these pea-shaped glands are responsible for keeping calcium at a normal level in our blood.

Because of calcium's important and widespread role throughout the body and because of its depressant effects in overdosage, people should be very careful they don't get too much of this vital chemical. They should be careful, too, about vitamin D. This substance promotes the absorption of calcium, thereby elevating its level in the bloodstream.

So, if you're giving your child megadoses of vitamin D, you may inadvertently be poisoning your child (and making him or her depressed at the same time). If you do give your children vitamins, read the labels carefully.

□

MEDICAL EXAMINATION

Just by looking at your child, your physician is likely to get a sense of just how ill he or she is.

Phrases like "minimally ill-looking," "healthy-appearing," and "chronically ill" cross the doctor's brain and strongly influence the degree testing to be carried out.

Something as simple as checking the height and weight can provide crucial information pertaining to a variety of disorders. These figures are plotted on graphs that show how your child compares with children of the same age.

Plotted over time—months to years—these graphs can show the doctor if your child has fallen off in growth. When it comes to disorders such as cancer, depression, and anorexia nervosa, such information is critical for diagnosis and management.

The remainder of the examination will be devoted to a thorough check of organ systems in which illness might cause or contribute to symptoms of depression. Your doctor is likely to consider such problems as sinusitis, asthma, ulcerative colitis, kidney disease, hepatitis, and infectious mononucleosis ("mono").

Medical Testing

Obviously, any investigation or testing your doctor wishes to carry out will be dictated by the medical disorders raised for consideration through the history and examination.

Testing may include blood tests such as levels of thyroid hormone and calcium, urine tests for sugar, stool examination for blood, and X rays of the gastrointestinal tract.

Referral to a gastroenterologist, endocrinologist, or other specialist may stem from your doctor's evaluation.

□

NEUROLOGIC CONDITIONS

It's scary, but the child with frequent headaches, poor concentration, and irritability could have a brain tumor.

Not only do the symptoms of depression and brain tumor overlap strikingly, but both problems usually become apparent quite slowly over time.

□

EVELYN

Evelyn was eleven years old when she was brought to see me by her mother. "She was irritable all the time," she said. Evelyn also had headaches up to three times weekly. They lasted a few hours at a time.

Her grades had worsened over the previous year. "She didn't get along with her brother or sister at all," her mother said. A bike accident and a fall resulting from her "rubbery-leggedness" prompted her mother to seek neurologic consultation.

I found Evelyn to be subdued though not depressed. Examination of her eyes showed extreme blurriness of the optic nerve heads (papilledema) that suggested a brain tumor, further indicated by her problems with coordination.

A CAT scan of her brain showed a large tumor. It proved to be malignant and could not be removed totally. She received radiation therapy and chemotherapy for several weeks before she died.

COMMENT. The story of this child illustrates how similar the symptoms of brain tumor and depression can be—worsened school performance, irritability, headaches.

You might say, "What difference did it make that she was diagnosed late, or even diagnosed at all? After all, it was a malignant tumor."

That's an important question. My response is twofold. First, roughly half the brain tumors in childhood are benign. One doesn't know for sure if a tumor is benign or malignant until it's operated upon.

The second point is exemplified by another patient of mine. This eleven-year-old boy also had frequent headaches. He was evaluated much earlier in his clinical course than Evelyn. He had only slight blurriness inside his eyes.

A CAT scan showed a tumor, which was subsequently believed to be totally removed during surgery. It was the same malignant type as with Evelyn. But six years later he is well and considered cured.

□

TESTING FOR BRAIN TUMORS

As we saw above, brain tumors in childhood can produce their effects slowly, insidiously. Not dramatically the way a tumor might announce itself in you or me, as adults—with a seizure.

The reason for that is location. Most pediatric brain tumors lie in the lowermost, back part of the skull. That's far from centers for language and voluntary movement. It's where the cerebellum is situated, a part of the brain involved in coordinating movement.

Unfortunately, tumors in children are often discovered almost by accident. By that point, they may have progressed so far that treatment is much more difficult. If the tumor is malignant, it may by that time have spread.

Your pediatrician has brain tumor in mind when he or she looks at your child's eyes with a special light called an ophthalmoscope. The doctor looks through the pupil—the black part of the eye—to the very back. That's where the optic nerve takes off, carrying vision to the brain.

The doctor is looking for papilledema. That's a swelling or blurriness of the part of the optic nerve visible through the pupil. A brain tumor can occur without this swelling. So a normal optic disk does not exclude the possibility of a brain tumor. You can, however, justifiably be relieved a bit if the doctor reports to you, "The disk margins are sharp. There's no papilledema."

The Miracle of CAT and MRI

If your pediatrician does think brain tumor is a possible cause for your child's problems, he or she may get a picture of your child's brain using a CAT scan or MRI scan. These miraculous tools virtually allow a look inside the brain.

CAT stands for computerized axial tomography. X-ray pictures are taken at different levels, or cuts. A computer then reconstructs these cuts to make detailed two-dimensional pictures of the brain. (I expect that three-dimensional pictures will be routinely available within a decade.)

To help certain brain structures stand out more clearly, a colorless liquid is injected into a vein. This liquid is a contrast medium though it is often called (inaccurately) dye. Some people may be allergic to this substance, so hospitals and CAT scan facilities keep antiallergy medicines on hand should they be needed.

MRI is magnetic resonance imaging. It does not involve radiation. Nor does it require an injection. Allergy is thus not an issue. It does require the subject to lie very still, for twenty to thirty minutes or so, compared with three to ten minutes for many CAT scans.

The pictures of the brain are generally somewhat more detailed with MRI than with CAT scanning. For that reason (plus its not involving radiation or injections) I usually prefer magnetic resonance imaging when available.

Before or after an imaging test, your doctor may wish to obtain neurologic consultation. If a tumor is present, you will, of course, be referred to a neurosurgeon.

To conclude the topic of brain tumors, you should keep it in mind that just because a person has ample reason to be depressed doesn't mean he can't have a brain tumor, too!

□

TOXIC CONDITIONS

Drugs are everywhere. There are those that are prescribed for legitimate medical or psychiatric purposes, and those that are used illicitly, outside the law.

Drugs are linked in several important ways with depression, especially during adolescence, when risk-taking, peer pressure, and rebelliousness move many toward behavior that is outright dangerous.

Drugs can cause symptoms of depression. They can be used to blunt or ward off depression. In either instance, they can pave the way toward suicide.

Categories of Drugs

Among the categories of drugs that are commonly abused are depressants and stimulants. Depressant drugs (some of them also known as sedatives) include alcohol, barbiturates, benzodiazepines (the family that includes Valium and Xanax), and the opiates (such as morphine, heroin, and meperidine, or Demerol).

Stimulant drugs include amphetamines and cocaine. After the "high" that such drugs induce, the user typically "crashes," entering a state of physiologic depression.

These drugs interfere with thinking and behavior through their acute actions. At least as important is their potential for bringing about addiction.

Addiction

Addiction is a complicated set of behaviors and responses that involves both physiological as well as psychological dependence.

Physiological dependence means that once a person has gotten used to a certain amount of the drug, that person's body *requires* that drug in order to prevent unpleasant withdrawal symptoms.

We all know people who have quit smoking cigarettes. Put in another way, they have withdrawn from physiological dependence upon nicotine. (At least that's the first part of the process.) We've all heard (or know firsthand) how hard the first week can be. Intense craving for tobacco and other physical symptoms make life miserable for a while.

But after that week, nicotine is out of the system and the person can move beyond physiological dependence to tackle what can be an even greater problem—psychological dependence. That's the almost ritualistic need to have the drug, like a security blanket, which may take weeks, months, or longer to break.

Fortunately for their health and that of their families, people succeed all the time in conquering physiological and psychological dependence.

Addiction *can* be treated effectively. Can it be cured? Without getting into a long discussion, I would say simply that in most instances it can be successfully managed. That success depends upon honest recognition of the problem, personal commitment, and skilled help.

Drugs and Your Child

As you observe the behavior of a child who has symptoms of depression, you should ask yourself, "Are drugs playing a role here?"

Remember that drugs can affect behavior in many ways. There are the acute effects—the drowsiness of sedatives, the agitation of stimulants. When drug use has reached the level of dependence, it brings out drug-seeking behaviors.

One of the most important is stealing. This can involve

taking money from parents, selling the family silverware, or breaking into shops to obtain goods for sale. If you encounter such behavior, keep the possibility of drug abuse—and underlying depression—in mind.

Problems with Prescribed Drugs

Less often, prescribed drugs used thoughtfully for legitimate purposes can cause or contribute to depression.

Phenobarbital, carbamazepine (Tegretol), and primidone (Mysoline) are anticonvulsant medications that may cause sleepiness and irritability. Because they may also cause clumsiness and incoordination, these drugs—in overdosage—may mimic the effects of brain tumor.

Sleepiness generally occurs when the level of medication in the bloodstream (and thus reaching the brain) is too high. There can be many reasons for this: physician error, pharmacist error, parent error, child error. (Don't forget the possibility of intentional overdosage!)

Sometimes the addition of a second medication drives up the level of the first. This occurs predictably when valproic acid (Depakene) is added to a regimen that includes phenobarbital. Measurement of anticonvulsant blood levels will usually identify overdosage.

Carbon Monoxide and Other Toxins

Other toxic influences should be considered as well. During winter months, when windows are kept closed and space heaters are in use, carbon monoxide poisoning can occur.

Carbon monoxide is a colorless and odorless gas that latches on to oxygen and doesn't let go. As a result, less oxygen reaches the brain. The effects—now well known to you as symptoms of depression—can include irritability, poor concentration, and headaches.

A simple blood test, measuring hemoglobin that's carrying carbon monoxide instead of oxygen, can determine if this is the problem.

Now that you've had a close look at the medical evaluation of your child, let's see how you and your doctor can best prepare your child for psychiatric consultation.

4

Preparing for Psychiatric Consultation

Once medical evaluation has been carried out, it's time to move ahead to consultation with a psychiatrist or other mental health professional. That will allow for the diagnosis of depression to be confirmed and a treatment plan established.

This is an important step, one which your doctor can greatly facilitate. There are also things that you should be aware of that can help a great deal. That's what this chapter is about.

The pediatrician may frame his approach to further evaluation in this way:

"Well, Mrs. Jones, I have thoroughly examined Betty. I have little doubt that your instincts are on target. I agree that we're probably dealing with a problem of depression.

"I feel it would be important to explore certain medical causes. Then Betty should see a psychiatrist or psychologist for consultation, someone who specializes in emotional problems of children.

"I don't want to take a shotgun approach and do every test in the book. With all her headaches, I'd like to exclude a brain tumor. We can do that with a CAT scan. And I'd like to rule out thyroid disorder or calcium deficiency by testing her blood.

"Because the change in Betty's behavior has been so drastic, I would like for her to be seen by a neurologist. Then, if all the tests are normal and the neurologist hasn't found anything to worry about, we should move ahead with psychiatric consultation."

□

WHAT PSYCHIATRIC CONSULTATION MEANS

The choice of the word "consultation" here is important and meaningful. When many people hear the word "psychologist" or "psychiatrist," they stiffen—"I'm not paying for twenty years on the couch!"

The kind of response probably stems from an outmoded notion of what psychiatry is about. A few decades ago, many people got the idea that three-to-five-time-per-week analysis was the only way psychiatry was practiced. Now there are many kinds of treatments to choose from.

Your child may be ready or reluctant to see a psychiatrist. Adolescents often bristle at any suggestion that they should see a mental health professional. "I'm not crazy," they assert. "You go. You're the one who needs it!"

On the other hand, your daughter or son may be eager to see a psychiatrist. A young woman whose depression started in early childhood told me recently: "When I was eleven my parents brought me to a dermatologist. She felt my rash was due to nerves and told my parents she thought I should 'see someone.'

"They weren't enthusiastic about this idea. I just about screamed out loud: 'Let me see someone! Let me see someone!'"

Unfortunately, that opportunity came a long, long time (and two suicide attempts) later!

Once you've decided that psychiatric consultation is needed, it's best to gain the support of your spouse as well. A united front may be crucial in getting your child the necessary help.

Remember that your job as parent is not to negotiate whether your son or daughter goes to see the psychiatrist. You've made that decision. Now it's a matter not of brute force but of salesmanship. To start with, that means getting some sort of acknowledgment that there is indeed a problem. You'd like your child's help in solving it.

You might take the following approach:

"Sara, you say you don't want to see a psychiatrist. You don't think it's necessary. But your father and I think that's a mistake.

"We're concerned about how you've been feeling lately. We're convinced it's important to look into emotional factors. And that's the job of a specialist."

What your pediatrician is suggesting is not psychoanalysis or even psychotherapy but, rather, consultation. This is a process of evaluation, directed towards establishing a diagnosis and treatment plan.

☐

CARRYING OUT
THE CONSULTATION

Consultation may be carried out by one (or a team) of several mental health professionals. A psychiatrist is a physician who specializes in disorders of thought, mood, and behavior. As a licensed physician, he is able to prescribe medication, should it be needed.

A psychologist is a nonmedical doctor also trained in the diagnosis and treatment of emotional and behavioral problems. If medication is an issue, the psychologist will call upon a psychiatric colleague for additional consultation.

A psychiatric social worker is another nonmedical specialist with postgraduate training in psychiatric diagnosis and therapy.

The consultation process generally involves one or several meetings with your child, his or her siblings, you, and your spouse. If you are separated or divorced, both parents should nonetheless plan on participating in the evaluation.

Don't hesitate to clarify financial aspects of the consultation. Check with the specialist's secretary prior to the visit or speak with the psychiatrist at the first meeting. Contact your insurance company if you have any questions about coverage, and bring any necessary forms with you.

The child, as well as you, should be aware that the purpose of these meetings is not to find someone to blame. You are all encouraged to share information, even "family secrets," that may help explain the changes in mood and behavior that prompted the consultation.

This process usually takes several weeks. It is concluded with a conference explaining the findings of the mental health professional or team. The written report sent to the referring physician may also be available to the parents.

□

CONCLUDING CONSULTATION

In concluding the consultation, the mental health professional will provide a statement of what he or she feels the problem to be—in others words, the diagnosis—and recommendations for treatment.

This should take place in a meeting with the child and both parents present. Everyone should have a chance to ask questions, both with everybody present and individually.

One of the possible outcomes of this meeting is the recommendation for no treatment. Instead, you may be advised to see what happens over several months and meet again at that time.

Over the past several years there has been an increased appreciation that many of a child's conflicts and other psychological-emotional hurdles are not in themselves pathologic.

Everyone has them to deal with. It's *how* you deal with them that matters. Modern psychiatry looks at these coping mechanisms as well as the bottom line—the person's feelings and functioning in his or her world—to formulate a diagnosis and treatment plan.

If you feel the specialist has missed the boat and failed to appreciate the seriousness of your situation, respond to your gut feeling. Get a second opinion. It should not be insulting to the first specialist.

Be prepared, though, to modify your position based on further observations of your child and input from the second specialist.

□

RECOMMENDATION FOR PSYCHOTHERAPY

A recommendation for psychotherapy may stem from the consultation process. This may take the form of individual meetings, family sessions, marital counseling, or group therapy.

Treatment with medication may be recommended to start at once. Or the suggestion may be made to reconsider it in several months. (See Chapter 5 for discussion of medication effects and indications for use.)

The psychiatrist who recommends therapy may not be in a position to provide that therapy. That can be tremendously disappointing for the child and parents. They may have entered the diagnostic process fearfully and tentatively only to come to like and trust the specialist.

To prevent this potentially upsetting outcome, make sure you and your child understand in advance the structure of the evaluation process—how many sessions, over what period of time, and possible outcomes.

Having gotten to know you, your child, and your family well over the preceding several weeks, your consultant is in an excellent position to recommend a therapist you are likely to work well with.

Another way to attain a good match between your child and a therapist is to get the names of several people from other parents. Your child may have a friend in therapy. If that has been a positive experience, by all means find out who that person is.

At this point, you're not dealing with an emergency. It's not like going to the emergency room in the middle of the night and having to accept the doctor on call, whoever that might be. Under the current circumstances, you and your child have the opportunity to select a therapist thoughtfully and carefully.

Your child should know that if things don't work out with the therapist you've started with—if the chemistry isn't right—you'll find another person that is suitable.

That doesn't mean an endless round of doctor shopping. What it does mean is that your child knows he or she isn't stuck should things not work out satisfactorily.

You might say to your child: Let me know if any of your friends has a therapist they've had a good experience with. I can then make an appointment, and we can meet him or her. If that doesn't work out, we'll find somebody else."

Remember that your job as parent is not to negotiate whether your son or daughter goes for therapy. You and your spouse make that decision. It's like any other important aspect of child care: the responsibility of an adult.

You should speak openly with your child about the consultant's diagnostic findings and recommendations for treatment. Your child *should* resist treatment if the problem and proposed help are not well explained.

Your child should know that it usually does take a while to get to know and trust a new therapist (if that will be the case). But therapy will offer an opportunity to discuss privately things that may be hard to talk about with parents, things that may be causing the unhappiness and emotional difficulties that have been so disturbing over weeks and months.

Once suitable explanation has been made, your child can be an active and willing participant in therapy, something which bodes well for its success.

Within the bounds of confidentiality, you should also enlist the support of siblings and other key relatives. It can be very hard for a child to enter therapy if a brother is making fun of it or if a favorite uncle is telling your son it's a waste of time.

What the psychiatrist does is the subject of the next chapter.

5

What the Psychiatrist Does

There's a great deal of confusion and misunderstanding about how a psychiatrist or other mental health professional goes about his or her business. I'd like to help you understand that before you bring your child to see this specialist for consultation.

The diagnostic process involves several parts. First is the gathering of information—history-taking. Next is the psychiatric examination. This is followed by organizing the information into a diagnostic formulation and treatment plan.

The final step is communicating that information to the child and parents so they will understand the problem and the choices for treatment. Then they can move ahead with knowledge and commitment to take steps that are likely to work best for them.

Now let's go through these steps in some detail.

□

GATHERING INFORMATION

The psychiatrist gets information in at least two ways. One is directly from the child and parents; the other is from outside sources (teachers, other doctors, previous therapists).

As with medical history-taking, the process begins with the child's and parents' perception of the problem: "Jimmy, can you tell me why you're here today?"

Sometimes that's enough to get the ball rolling. If necessary, the psychiatrist can be more specific: "What seems to be troubling you lately?"

The Child's Own Words

Questioning will often proceed in a nondirective manner. That is, the child is asked to tell her story, in her own words, in her own order. In that way, the psychiatrist not only finds out what is bothering the child—from the child's perspective—but also gets a sense of the child's awareness, intelligence, organization, and emotional state.

Dr. Anderson: "What seems to be the problem lately, Jessica?"

Jessica: "I don't have the energy to do anything, even things I usually like to do."

Dr. Anderson: "Tell me about it."

Jessica: "I don't know what to say."

Dr. Anderson: "Anything you like."

Jessica: "Well, it's bad. Because my friends wonder what's wrong with me and I don't know."

Dr. Anderson: "What do you think is wrong?"

Jessica: "My mother thinks I'm depressed."

Dr. Anderson: "What do *you* think is wrong?"

Jessica: "I don't know. But I sure feel bad."

Dr. Anderson: "What do you mean 'bad'?"

Jessica: "It's hard to say. It feels like I'm always angry. Even if there's no reason. When my brother says something to me, I want to bite his head off. And I'm always screaming at my mother."

As you can see from this line of questioning, the specialist has gently entered into an area of crucial importance—Jessica's mood, her overall emotional state.

Further discussion may include the child's understanding of when she started feeling angry and what she thought her anger was due to.

Speaking with the Child Alone

You can see why it's important for the psychiatrist to speak with the child alone (at least at some point in the diagnostic process).

Dr. Anderson: "Have you had any problem with your sleep lately?"

Jessica: "Yes. I can't get to sleep."

Dr. Anderson: "What do you mean?"

Jessica: "I lie down but I have trouble falling asleep."

Dr. Anderson: "Why is that?"

Jessica: "I don't know."

Dr. Anderson: "Do you think of things when you lie down and try to fall asleep?"

Jessica: "Yes."

Dr. Anderson: "Like what?"

Jessica: "A lot of things."

Dr. Anderson: "What's one?"

Jessica: "I'm kind of worried my parents are going to get a divorce."

Notice what the psychiatrist has done with the subject of possible sleep disturbance. First, he confirmed there was a sleep problem—as you know, one of the symptoms of depression.

Then, in the course of learning what kind of sleep difficulty, he found out what was very troubling to Jessica, the threatened divorce of her parents. That certainly contributed to her mood disturbance, the anger she described earlier.

You should notice again that the psychiatrist proceeds very gently. He starts with the child's current life events. He seeks to understand what the child is experiencing *now*. He then tries to understand why.

Dealing with intensely personal matters, the child and

parents have to establish a certain level of confidence and trust before such material is chared.

You can see why psychiatric consultation may take sever al sessions. This is in contrast to neurologic consultation, for example, which is often a single meeting.

□

CONFIDENTIALITY

Confidentiality is important in all of medicine. It is particularly important in psychiatry. Your child's psychiatrist will not without your permission speak with your child's teachers, previous therapists, or other parties.

Dr. Anderson: "Jessica, I'd like you to know that the things we'll be speaking about are confidential. They'll stay between you and me. I'm not going to tell your parents what we talk about unless I ask you first and you tell me it's okay."

You and your child are encouraged to share important and personal information with the psychiatrist. But you should be aware—I know this may sound funny—that the psychiatrist is not a mind reader, hypnotist, or manipulator, pulling things from you that you don't wish to divulge.

The mental health professional is specially trained to make you comfortable, to gain your trust. Once that has been established, you will be better able to share information and feelings that may have been very, very difficult to talk about previously.

Your purpose in doing so now, if you choose to, is to help solve your child's problems.

You Don't Have to Answer

If there are things that are too personal to get into now, you have a right not to discuss them.

Dr. Anderson: "You had a similar experience when you were a child?"

Mrs. Stevens: "Yes."

Dr. Anderson: "Can you tell me about that?"

Mrs. Stevens: "I'd rather not. Not right now."

Dr. Anderson: "Have you spoken with anyone about those experiences?"

Mrs. Stevens: "No, I never have."

Dr. Anderson: "Well, if you'd like to, I'd be pleased to meet with you and discuss them. Or I can suggest someone you might speak with. Now, let's move ahead to something else."

A First Step

The psychiatrist has seemingly stumbled upon an important issue. Mrs. Stevens had been sexually abused as a child. That may have some relevance to her own daughter. It certainly has relevance to her own life.

But that's something that has been so disturbing to her that she's never told anyone. This is the first step toward her dealing with it in an adult, therapeutic setting.

The psychiatrist is not pushing, though. He recognizes the intensely personal and painful nature of the subject and the need for Mrs. Stevens to move forward at her own pace.

It is, of course, not really a matter of stumbling. The skilled mental health professional knows that many of us have had difficult experiences and profoundly troubling feelings that may be buried deep within us.

The professional also knows that some of these issues would likely benefit from exposure to the light of an adult day in a therapeutic context. Other things should be left alone. The experienced therapist can help decide the right course of action.

As you can tell, when you bring your child to see a psychiatrist, you may find that you, too, could have benefited from therapy. How many times have I had a parent come back a year or two after I've referred his or her child for psychiatric consultation and treatment to tell me: "I wish I'd seen someone when I was younger!"

But, there's no time like the present. So, if you think you'd like to pursue consultation for yourself, by all means do it. It can be a rewarding pursuit. It may be long overdue.

□

MAKING A TIME LINE

Some of the problems with mood and behavior in childhood occur episodically. In order to gain a better sense of the time course, the specialist may ask you to make a time line.

This involves plotting major events in your child's life on a piece of paper (often, several strung together). On it you indicate periods of abnormal mood, normal mood, important experiences, and medication use (if any). This can be invaluable in identifying stresses that might be causing or contributing to your child's depression.

□

OTHER MEMBERS OF THE TEAM

Part of the information-gathering process may be carried out by a social worker, psychologist, or other member of the intake team. Their information will be shared with the psychiatrist (or other team leader) to help in the formulation of a diagnosis and treatment plan.

Certain questions will come up that may be sensitive. For example, it is important to know if there are family members with a history of mental or emotional illness.

Since your response may involve discussing your own depression—or a brother who committed suicide—this part of the interview is best carried out with the child out of the room.

The family history can be extremely valuable in your child's assessment. Let's say your aunt has been diagnosed as being manic-depressive and has done well with lithium treatment. That can provide a clue to your teenager's angry and aggressive behavior and a specific drug to consider if medication is to be used.

As part of the information-gathering process, records may also be obtained from outside sources. With your signed permission, the psychiatrist can request previous hospital, school, and psychologic testing reports.

□

THE PSYCHIATRIST'S ROLE

The psychiatrist doesn't learn by just asking questions or requesting records. He or she takes in crucial information by watching, listening, and feeling emphathically.

I like to tell medical students about lessons I've learned in my own study and practice of medicine.

One of the things a doctor soon becomes aware of when dealing with children is that his very presence may be upsetting to them. The child's distress may interfere with how the doctor views the child. It may even destroy the opportunity to carry out a useful examination.

With that in mind, I tell my students that "It took three years of pediatric training for me to learn to keep my hands off patients.

"Make your observations first. Resist the urge to 'be a doctor' by putting the cold stethoscope on the child's chest and pinning him down to look at his ears.

"And"—what I consider to be the most valuable lesson—
"keep your mouth shut" (something it took me a year of
training in child psychiatry to learn).

It's not just the laying on of hands that's a form of intervention. Speaking is a kind of intervention, too, in dealing
with a depressed child.

Tuning in to the Child

I don't mean that I, my students, or a psychiatrist should be a
sphinx, sitting silently nearby, with an occasional nod of
agreement or acknowledgment.

What I suggest is that by remaining relatively quiet, listening, and observing, the physician can get a sense of what
channel the patient is tuned in to and what messages he or
she is broadcasting.

When the doctor asks a specific question, he's doing the di-
aling, controlling the conversation. If the child selects the
channel and starts talking about her beloved dog who just
got run over by a car, that's significant. That's what's on her
mind *now*.

Understanding what the child is experiencing helps to establish rapport and builds toward other important areas of
discussion.

It's true that she may be anxious about seeing a psychiatrist. Her parents may have primed her to talk about "meaningful" things. But over the course of several diagnostic-con-
sultative sessions, a psychiatrist can gain a remarkably full
understanding of the rich and fascinating undercurrents of
your child's emotional life.

An Emotional Sounding Board

Just as the the pediatrician has his own tools—the stethoscope, tongue depressor, otoscope—the psychiatrist has his tools as well. One of the most important is himself.

By that I mean the psychiatrist uses himself as a sounding board to get a direct sense of your child's emotional state.

This is not as mysterious as it might seem. You probably do it all the time. You walk into a room. You feel tension in the air. Or you describe other situations: "The gloom was so thick you could cut it with a knife." "She was so sad she made me feel like crying."

These are all examples of how mood, particularly depression, can have a contagious quality. It's this feature of depression (as well as other moods) that the mental health professional is sensitive to and uses to identify your child's emotional state.

Your child may make you depressed, too. That doesn't necessarily mean he or she is depressed. You may be upset about something else going on in your life. You may be projecting your own feelings onto your child.

Although you may have gone down the depression checklist point by point, the psychiatrist taking a history and examining your child does not generally go down a list.

At some point, though, he or she is likely to use such a standardized list of symptoms. But too much is to be gained by letting things flow during much of the evaluation to merely check things off on a form.

□

PICTURE DRAWING

Many children are not comfortable or experienced in speaking about emotional matters. One way the psychiatrist has to get around this problem—particularly with preschool and school-aged children (three to twelve years)—is through pictures. She simply asks your child to draw a picture of himself or herself.

Children also love to draw their families (including their pets). A great deal can be learned about important relationships from these drawings.

In my pediatric days, I evaluated an eight-year-old boy because he had had frequent bowel accidents and behavior problems over several months. While I spoke with his mother, he drew a picture of himself and his family as I had requested.

In his picture, Jimmy stood on the deck of a ship. On its side was written "Titanic." The caption read: "Look out! Iceberg ahead!"

This boy's problems began when his father was killed in an automobile crash six months earlier. This was understandably a very upsetting event, something he'd had difficulty discussing.

His picture showed how actively the death of his father was concerning him, even though he was unwilling or unable to talk about it. I referred him to a psychiatrist so he could deal more effectively with his problems.

Just asking the child to "draw a picture of anything; here's some paper and a box of markers" can provide extremely valuable information, and avenues of further discussion and exploration.

Issues and events that the child finds too difficult or painful to speak about can appear in such free drawings. The five-year-old child whose family picture shows her teenaged brother with prominent genitals is making a statement that may have relevance to her behavior disturbance.

□

FREE PLAY

The psychiatrist can learn a great deal about what's going on in a child's mind through observing so-called free play. A doll house and puppets representing members of a family give the child a chance to enact scenes from his or her life. The specialist observes the activity and may ask questions about what's going on.

Specialist: "Joanna, who's that puppet?"

Joanna: "That's my Daddy."

Specialist: "And who's that?"

Joanna: "My Mommy."

Specialist: "What are they doing?"

Joanna: "They're arguing."

Specialist: "About what?"

Joanna: "Daddy stayed out late, and Mommy wants to know if he's been drinking again."

Specialist: "What happens next?"

Joanna: "They shout at each other and sometimes fight."

Specialist: "With their fists or just with words?"

Joanna: "Sometimes they hit."

Specialist: "How does that make you feel?"

Joanna: "Scared. I can't stand it when they fight."

Specialist: "What do you do when they fight?"

Joanna: "I go to my room to get away but I still listen."

COMMENT. In this situation, Joanna's aggressive puppet play led the specialist to inquire as to who was doing what to whom. That led to important information about physical violence between her parents and her father's apparent alcohol problem. Both issues had direct bearing on her depression, which she had been reluctant to speak about.

□

EDUCATED GUESSING

The psychiatrist is not going to ask a teenager to play with dolls. And asking an adolescent to draw a picture is likely to result in crossed arms and defiant refusal.

With adolescents, the psychiatrist will call upon other techniques. One important approach can be termed the "educated guess."

The psychiatrist has faced this situation before—dealing with a verbally uncommunicative adolescent, angry and mistrustful. The first thing to do is to establish rapport.

Getting inside the teenager's head through educated guesses based on experience can be an important first step in establishing rapport.

Psychiatrist: "I know you don't want to be here. Your parents dragged you here against your will. We haven't had a chance to speak much together. But I get the feeling things have been pretty miserable for you lately."

Breaking the Ice

After a bit of such one-way discussion with the teenager, a thaw may occur.

Instead of looking down in anger, the teenager, still withholding eye contact, may show signs of listening. This may progress to a nod of acknowledgment; later, outright words and perhaps even meaningful conversation. That may, however, wait until a future session when a sense of trust has been more firmly established.

The message getting through is that somebody understands (or is trying to understand). Somebody cares. Help is possible.

□

PROJECTIVE TESTING

For children of any age, projective tests can be used to gain knowledge of deep thoughts and feelings a child may not acknowledge or even be aware of. Such testing may be particularly helpful in gaining a better understanding of a child's depression.

Projective testing is carried out by a psychologist specifically trained in administering and interpreting such tests.

One projective test involves the child's viewing a set of pictures and making up a story about each one. For example, one picture is of a boy with a somber facial expression looking into a mirror.

Another projective test is the famous inkblot, or Rorschach, test. The child looks at a series of inkblots and tells the psychologist his or her responses.

Having a child "draw a picture of anything" is really a kind of projective test. The picture often reflects the content of the child's current consciousness.

Keep in mind that in such tests, the child projects emotions and concerns that may be conscious or unconscious upon the artistic creation. This projection allows the psychiatrist or psychologist to get a better handle on the ideas and feelings running through the child's mind at the time.

□

MORE ON THE PSYCHIATRIC EXAMINATION

There is quite a bit more to the psychiatric examination. In fact, it is remarkable how much the skilled mental health professional is taking in while seeming to be doing nothing—

listening, nodding, asking a question here and there.

In listening to your child without providing a great deal of structure, the psychiatrist gains a sense of the flow and connectedness of ideas within the child's mind.

If your child is very distractible, the conversation may jump around a great deal due to noises in the office or outside.

Your child may be distracted by the *sound* of his own words. That's what connects one idea with another rather than the meaning of the words. In that situation, your child may have a thought disorder in addition to, or instead of, a mood disorder.

☐

LAPSES IN CONVERSATION

Lapses in the conversation may have several meanings. Your child may have come up against a particularly painful or difficult topic and be unwilling or unable to continue.

He or she may be having a seizure, manifested in a staring spell. He or she may be hearing voices or having visual hallucinations.

☐

DELUSIONS

Sometimes depressed children will have delusions. A delusion is a false belief that's firmly held onto despite what should be convincing evidence to the contrary.

Your daughter might feel, for example: "I'm too fat." You know from looking at her and reviewing your pediatrician's charts that, if anything, she's on the slender side.

If your daughter persists in sticking to that view of herself despite looking in the mirror and discussing the matter with her doctor, that qualifies as a delusion. She may well have anorexia nervosa, a disorder that is often associated with depression.

□

LOSS OF INTELLECTUAL FUNCTION

In the course of examining your child, the psychiatrist is also getting a sense of memory. Has there been a falloff? Is it associated with depressing events? Or has there been a gradual decline over several years?

Memory disturbance can be prominent with depression. It may have led to academic failure, something that prompted your concern in the first place. The psychiatrist may wonder if memory disturbance is associated with a deterioration in intellectual status.

If such a falloff is suspected, further consultation may be recommended. A psychologist may be asked to carry out psychometric (IQ) testing to see just what the measured intelligence level is. In this situation, previous IQ testing for comparison would be extremely valuable.

You may be referred back to your pediatrician or a neurologist to look into identifiable organic causes for the memory loss.

□

PULLING IT ALL TOGETHER

Sometimes a single meeting with a mental health specialist can lead to a diagnosis. "I agree with you 100 percent, Mrs. Johnson. Your child is depressed. This is what I recommend you do now. . . . "

Most of the time, the evaluation process involves several

meetings, and perhaps several team members as well. After all members of the team have had a chance to evaluate the child and family from their own perspectives, they may meet as a group in a diagnostic conference to exchange findings, ideas, and recommendations.

Or, they may submit their reports to the team leader, who pulls the information together to arrive at a diagnostic and therapeutic formulation.

A Kind of Commencement

The meeting with the psychiatrist is very much like a commencement. It's the end of something—the process of diagnostic consultation. But, more important than that, it's also the beginning—a time when your fuzzy notions of what's been going on with your child have been sharpened and you're ready to establish a treatment plan to get him or her well again.

It's important that both the parents and the child take part in this meeting and that everyone have the opportunity to speak with the psychiatrist without other family members present.

The goal of the meeting is for everyone—child included—to understand what the problem is and what the choices for treatment are. With that kind of understanding, the chances for a successful outcome are maximized.

☐

THE BENEFIT OF KNOWLEDGE

It can be a great relief to know there's a name for what your child has been going through—depression. It's not just a nameless, diffuse force exerting its unpleasant effects in so many ways.

Children are exquisitely sensitive to feelings of being abnormal. Your child should know that feelings of depression are decidedly normal. Having a depressive disorder isn't normal, but then again neither is having an earache.

Both get better with the right kind of treatment. You wouldn't want to let the earache go without proper diagnosis and treatment. Your child might wind up with a perforated eardrum and permanent hearing loss.

You made the same kind of decision when it came to your child's mood disorder. You opted for proper diagnosis. Now you're ready to pursue the appropriate treatment.

The value of knowing the diagnosis was brought home to me by a seven-year-old girl I evaluated who had a bizarre form of migraine.

She was anxious about moving out of state with her family. That brought on a peculiar memory disturbance that was more distressing to her than the headache that was associated.

Once she learned she was not losing her mind and that the "weird" tricks her brain was playing on her were due to migraine, she was immensely relieved. With a few trips to her new home and further discussions with her parents, her migraines disappeared.

☐

INPATIENT EVALUATION

Sometimes the initial diagnostic assessment will be done on an inpatient basis, that is, with your child hospitalized. This may be necessary if he or she is considered suicidal, violent, or dangerously unpredictable, and it appears too risky to pursue evaluation over several weeks as an outpatient.

Many depressed persons have suicidal thoughts but are unlikely to act on them. They do not require hospitalization unless there are other concerns, such as limited supervision at home, that make it advisable.

Others have made serious attempts to kill themselves, have made detailed plans to do so, or are impulsive and unpredictable. Hospitalization provides necessary protection while the seriousness of the problem is being evaluated, contributing causes sought, and a treatment plan established.

Carrying out psychiatric assessment on an inpatient basis has another great advantage. You can get a remarkably detailed picture within a relatively short period of time, often a week or two rather than a month or longer.

It can be valuable to clarify for the child and family that he or she is not being institutionalized. Rather, the child and family are told that a further diagnostic assessment is being sought in a specialized psychiatric unit, which may take several weeks to, occasionally, a few months.

□

RECOMMENDATIONS

There are many possible outcomes to the diagnostic process. One is that the psychiatrist does not feel he or she has reached a clear diagnosis. In that case, additional evaluation may be requested, on an outpatient or inpatient basis.

Recommendations may include individual psychotherapy, family therapy, or parent guidance. These are discussed in the next chapter.

It's important to keep in mind that the depressed child is not necessarily the "sickest" person in the family. He might not even be "sick" at all—merely reacting to major stresses such as parental alcoholism, marital separation, or sexual abuse.

Antidepressant medication may be recommended at the time consultation is concluded. Or the suggestion may be to reconsider it once an ongoing relationship between child and therapist has been established.

☐

WHAT YOU SHOULD NOW KNOW

By the end of the evaluation phase, you should know a great deal:

The nature of your child's problems. The diagnosis. Interrelated problems in other family members—including yourself—that may be contributing to your child's difficulties.

What treatment (or combination of treatments) should be helpful in getting your child well as soon as possible. What the cost of these proposed treatments might be. How long you can anticipate the healing process will take.

You are not expected to understand and digest everything you are told at the diagnostic conference. Taking notes, having your pediatrician with you, and studying a copy of the diagnostic report are measures that can greatly aid your understanding.

You and your spouse may need a few feedback sessions with the psychiatrist to make sure you understand the diagnosis and treatment recommendations and to work out a treatment plan given the options presented.

☐

A DIFFERENT VIEW

You may disagree with the diagnosis and recommendations. Maybe the psychiatrist and his colleagues felt your child was not depressed. Or perhaps they felt he was very, very depressed—and required immediate hospitalization!

It's important for you to tell the psychiatrist what you

think and why. Your spouse and your child may or may not agree with you and should be given the opportunity to discuss their views as well.

Having entrusted your child to the care of the psychiatrist and his or her fellow professionals, you must make sure you understand what it is they're saying and what their reasons are.

There is often room and reason for thoughtful disagreement. As a parent, however, your view of things may be biased by your wish that things were better, not so serious.

Once your child has made a serious attempt to kill herself, for example, that fact can never be blinked away (although it doesn't have to remain in the forefront of your daily consciousness).

If you still have disagreements and concerns after you have a full understanding of the diagnosis and treatment brought forward by the psychiatrist, then by all means get a second opinion.

The next two chapters will be devoted to the treatment of depression in children and adolescents.

6

Treatment of Depression

Your suspicion of depression has been confirmed. You've got a plan to help your child.

How will the depression be treated? That's the focus of this chapter.

To review for a minute, by this point you've clarified at least one very important thing. You're dealing with depression the *disorder*, not merely depression the *symptom*.

One is a sustained, interfering mood (or emotional state). The other is a passing reaction, unpleasant as it may be, to a personal experience.

□

KINDS OF TREATMENT

Treatment for depression in childhood and adolescence can take one or more of several forms. These include individual therapy, educational assistance, family therapy, group therapy, and parental guidance.

There are things, too, that you have learned from your everyday experience in handling your own emotions that you can put to use in helping your child.

Medication and its possible role are discussed in the next chapter.

□

INDIVIDUAL THERAPY

Individual therapy involves your child and a mental health specialist. He or she may be a psychiatrist, psychologist, social worker, psychiatric nurse, or other trained and qualified professional.

Meetings are generally weekly, occasionally more often during initial stages of treatment. Sessions usually last from forty-five minutes to an hour, considerably less for younger children.

What goes on in therapy? There's no set routine; each case has its own scenario.

In general, the therapist begins with what's happening in the child's life. From there, he or she explores what your child is feeling, why, and what—if anything—might be done about it.

□

STACIE

Stacie was fifteen years old when her family moved to Massachusetts so her father could pursue a graduate degree in engineering. She was excited about the move but sorry to leave her friends and old, familiar neighborhood.

At her new school, things seemed strange and different. She didn't feel like participating in extracurricular activities.

She just came home, went to her room, and slept. Sometimes right through supper. She often felt on the verge of tears for no reason at all.

Her brothers and sisters teased her by calling her "one of the Seven Dwarfs"—Sleepy or Grumpy.

No One to Turn To

She knew something was wrong. But there didn't seem to be anyone to turn to for help. Her parents were busy. She had some new friends. But she didn't feel she knew them well enough to discuss anything very personal.

Meanwhile, things were getting worse, not better. And she didn't know what to do.

She rarely felt like going to school and was absent frequently. One day she stayed home while her mother visited a friend. Her father was at the university as usual.

"I felt very tired. I thought a warm bath might make me feel better. While I was lying there, I saw my father's razor and—I don't know why—I cut my wrist.

"I watched the blood trickle into the water. Then I must have passed out, because the next thing I knew my mother was opening the bathroom door.

"My parents were really upset. Scared. I saw my father cry for the first time."

Stacie was hospitalized for several weeks in the adolescent unit of a psychiatry service. She took part in individual therapy sessions with a social worker. Her parents came in for family meetings. Upon discharge, she was to continue seeing the social worker once a week.

Meetings with the Therapist

She found the meetings both interesting and helpful. "We just talk about what's going on," Stacie said. "Like if I'm down about something, we'll try to figure out why and what to do about it.

"I don't feel like I did before I went to the hospital. I haven't even thought of doing anything to hurt myself."

Continuing work done in the hospital, she explored further the feelings that led her to injure herself.

"I don't think I really wanted to kill myself," she said. "I was depressed. Things were so terrible. I missed my old friends a lot! I wanted to go back, but I knew I couldn't.

"I felt very alone, and I didn't know what to do.

"That was kind of stupid [cutting my wrists]. I wasn't thinking. I'm more patient now. I'm making some new friends and I just started a job after school.

"Having someone to talk to helps. I can now recognize strong feelings in myself I never knew existed. "I think I communicate better with my parents. But there are things I can discuss with my social worker I can't discuss with them.

"If things start going really bad in my life, I know to go and ask for help."

COMMENT. Stacie's story illustrates how profoundly upsetting a family move can be. Her depressive syndrome led to a serious suicide attempt.

Things appear to have worked out well, though, through the efforts of her therapist, her parents, and herself.

Her therapist provided a great deal of support during the period of hospitalization and beyond. The depression that led to the suicide attempt did not disappear. But now it was out in the open and its causes could be sought and dealt with.

Her parents were understanding and patient. They did not, however, tiptoe around her for fear of triggering another suicide attempt. Family meetings were helpful in facilitating communication and ensuring that there would not be inappropriate manipulation.

Stacie could now recognize different degrees of depression in herself. She knew what to do about it, too—something which should stand her in good stead in future years.

This story also shows how, particularly with an adolescent, isolation and withdrawal can lead to a buildup of bad, in fact unbearable, feelings. Such a buildup can have a fatal outcome. Fortunately, it was avoided here.

☐

PLAY OR PLAY THERAPY

With children younger than Stacie, treatment may take the form of play therapy.

This is one of the more mysterious and misunderstood aspects of child psychiatry. It's also one of its most wonderful in the helpful insights it offers into the working of the child's mind and the help it can provide.

Parents may get the idea that all their child does while they sit in the waiting room is draw pictures and play checkers.

That may be true as far as it goes. But there's a potentially important role for these activities beyond what might be readily apparent.

Drawing pictures can be a valuable way for the therapist to tap into some of the fantasies, fears, and feelings a child cannot or will not talk about.

Playing checkers can provide a pleasant, nonthreatening backdrop for conversation about other, more meaningful things.

Therapist: "Do you ever play checkers at home?"

Frederick: "I used to."

Therapist: "What do you mean?"

Frederick: "I used to. But I don't anymore."

Therapist: "Why is that?"

Frederick: "My brother always beats me."

Therapist: "And . . . ?"

Frederick: "And I can't stand that! It makes me mad!"

Therapist: "What do you feel like when you're mad?"

Frederick: "I feel like destroying him. That's for sure!"

In that way the therapist has opened up for discussion two important areas—Frederick's anger and his relationship with his brother.

The therapist doesn't have a rigid agenda to impose on the child. He uses his professional skills and knowledge to guide the conversation into areas that are important for the child.

□

HOW THERAPY HELPS

How does therapy help? In several ways.

First of all, it can provide a way of validating the child's reality. Children tend to view their parents as all-powerful and always right. They may be confused when they see their parents act in ways that are less than perfect.

In a therapy session, the child can run an everyday situation by the therapist and get a sense of whether the parent's actions were reasonable or inappropriate.

For example, a child might feel bitterly that she is being slighted in favor of her younger brother. In simply understanding the emotional upset the child has been experiencing, the therapist can make the child feel better.

She can then, with the help of the therapist, explore issues of favoritism and sibling rivalry in a constructive manner.

Speaking for the Child

If it's appropriate, the therapist may share some of the child's concerns with her parents. She might, for example, act as advocate for the child at a family meeting.

By getting the issues out on the table for discussion, the therapist helps make sure that a child's feelings are not allowed to stay buried and exert their depressing, constricting influence any longer.

Support

Support is another important aspect of therapy. Children who have been depressed know that their irritability and moodiness have probably cost them some friends.

As they get better, they may benefit from the support and encouragement of the therapist to get back into their old circle of friends or to make new ones.

Patience is an essential ingredient in the treatment of depression. A depressed child wants to wake up the next morning and feel totally well. It doesn't happen that dramatically, however. It takes time.

The therapist seeing the child weekly can point out ways he or she is improving and can support the child in being patient if progress feels too slow.

Unbottling Emotion

Merely expressing difficult and unpleasant feelings of depression, such as anger and sadness, can be helpful for the child.

Particularly when the child comes from a home where expressing emotion is taboo, sounding off in the therapist's office can keep these feelings from being bottled up indefinitely.

Keeping feelings inside can take a great deal of energy and can exert a negative influence upon the child's behavior and personality for years.

We all know persons who smile all the time. It doesn't take a psychoanalyst to know they may be seething with anger.

The child can learn in therapy that it's okay to be angry.

"You don't have laser beams in your eyes," a therapist told a nine-year-old boy. "You can't kill your mother by looking at her when you're angry."

Obviously, the therapist is not recommending the child "let it all hang out" when it comes to emotional expression. The child can explore in therapy ways of expressing anger and other emotions in ways that are acceptable.

□

EDUCATIONAL ASSISTANCE

School is a major part of the lives of all children and adolescents for many years. It's not surprising, then, that academic difficulties can have depressing effects upon a child.

Children have different abilities, different degrees of motivation, and different expectations placed upon them by their parents. A mismatch among these elements can generate a great deal of stress that may be expressed as depression.

For example, a child with average ability should be considered to be doing satisfactorily if he achieves at an average level academically, well if he does above-average work.

If his parents expect their son to be at the top of his class, however, trouble is likely. The boy may try hard to meet these expectations, staying up late working, doing assignments on weekends when his classmates are at the football game, giving up sports to spend more time on his studies.

Or he may decide his parents are "all wet"—totally unrealistic in their expectations. His response: complete refusal to participate in academics. The result: instead of getting C's and B's, it's all F's.

Either scenario can lead to a variety of physical or emotional difficulties. Problems may include chronic fatigue, weight loss, and irritability—all of them symptoms of depression.

The therapist is in an excellent position to understand what the child is feeling, why he is feeling that way, and what realistically can be done about it. Again, establishment of improved communication between child and parents is most helpful in dealing with the stressful academic pictures painted above.

□

FAMILY THERAPY

The depressed child or adolescent is not an island apart from others.

One of the most important facets of the child's life is as a member of a family. When it comes to therapy, the family can play a major role in helping the depressed child get better.

The family can be a major source of support to the child. The participation of family members in therapy meetings can be very helpful to the therapist as well as to the family.

She can directly observe interactions between family members. She can try to gain each of their perspectives on problems that are presented for discussion. In that way, she can help family members find ways to help each other within the office and beyond.

It is important that siblings know that all of you—not just the depressed child—are dealing with a problem that has a name: depression.

It's a problem that has to do with mood—a colorless, odorless, tasteless emotional force that strongly influences a person and those around him.

Opportunity for Learning

Family therapy sessions offer an ideal opportunity for other children in the family to learn to recognize symptoms of depression.

Recognizing symptoms of depression in their brother or sister, children will understand—without jealousy or anger—why their parents are "going easy" on Janet for a while. Not forever, just until she feels better.

"That's only natural," one child explained to me, "because that's what you'd expect if a person had bad asthma or some other illness."

The Right to Take It Easy

It's reasonable and appropriate for a depressed person to take it easy when she's not feeling well. The child should not feel guilty about functioning below her usual level.

Nor should she be made to feel worse by brothers and sisters bugging her because they think she's "getting away with murder"—not participating in family chores or keeping her room as neat as usually expected.

On the other hand, it would certainly not be appropriate for family members to tiptoe around the depressed child. A skilled family therapist can help parents sort out the right kind of balance for their family.

□

GROUP THERAPY

Group therapy for the depressed child can provide an opportunity to meet others who have experienced some of the same feelings. That can be very reassuring for children, who tend to feel "weird" or "different"—as if they're the only ones who've ever been depressed!

□

PARENTAL GUIDANCE

Particularly when a younger child is involved, a significant part of the treatment may involve just the parents and the therapist. Sessions are not a matter of the therapist's laying down the law or pontificating.

These meetings can take the form of problem-solving sessions, with a lot of give-and-take among parents and professional. For example, the father might feel his depressed son is ready to take on more in the way of household chores. His wife disagrees.

If they cannot come to an agreement outside the therapy session, that's a problem they can address at that time.

Father: "I think Jimmy should get back into the swing of things and take out the garbage on weekends like he used to."

Mother: "I disagree. That's when he needs to catch up on sleep. He's been pushing himself so hard just to get through the school day, he's exhausting himself."

Father: "The other children complain he's getting away with murder. They've been pretty understanding up to this point. I don't see why we can't ask this one simple thing of him."

Mother: "I just think it would be too much."

Therapist: "Maybe there's another chore, later in the day, that Jimmy could do."

Father: "Like?"

Mother: "What about feeding the cat and changing the kitty litter?"

Father: "Sounds okay. Let's bring it up this evening after supper."

□

DIVORCE

One of the issues that may come up in family meetings or parent guidance sessions is divorce. Divorce, separation, or marital difficulties that might lead to divorce—involving real or threatened loss—are common and important causes for depression in children and adolescents.

These issues are likely to be touched upon in a child's indi vidual therapy sessions as well.

Children tend to have the magical feeling that they caused their parents' breakup—something they did (like get in trouble, which caused a major argument) or didn't do (like get straight A's on their report card).

When parents split apart, the child must often contend with two major losses: a parent (since custody is rarely split down the middle, or felt as such) and self-esteem (the feeling being "If I weren't such a bad person, this wouldn't have happened").

Viewed Against the Alternative

At first blush, people outside the family almost universally regard divorce as bad for the children. It can, indeed, be depressing.

But, what outsiders don't know and what can probably never be known with certainty, is how bad the intact family was. The children may, in fact, be in a much better situation if they are no longer living with an abusive parent, for example.

The Child Who Is Too Good

Tears, sadness, and anger in the context of separation or divorce may signal a depressive reaction.

When these are absent, parents may sometimes breathe more easily than they should. Sometimes a child who seems to be handling things fine may not, in truth, be doing so well.

□

□
KAREN

Karen, nine years old, appeared to be doing well after her parents' divorce three months earlier. She was a "model child" at school and at home.

Her six-year-old brother made things difficult for Karen's mother. He was constantly fighting and crying. His pediatrician called it "an adjustment reaction."

COMMENT. A young woman depressed as a child told me: "Beware of the child who is too good. She may be trying to ward off depression."

I think that's exactly what was going on with Karen. She probably feared that if she were anything other than perfect, her mother would get angry and leave. She had already lost her father. She couldn't afford to lose anyone else!

□
THERAPY FOR PARENTS, TOO

Sometimes the best therapy for the child is therapy for a parent. Since disorders of mood often run in families, it is not uncommon for a depressed child to have a parent with major depression or anxiety.

A depressed mother or father is not likely to be well suited for providing the support, encouragement, and patience needed by the depressed child, who may be irritable, angry, or otherwise unhappy.

□
LENNY

Lenny was a nine-year-old boy I saw because of "headaches and other stuff," as he expressed it. The headaches proved to be infrequent and not very severe. It was the "other stuff" that was the really painful thing in his life: his emotional suffering.

The merest mention of his pet dog, who was run over and killed some six months earlier, made Lenny redden and burst into tears. That wasn't the only loss he had experienced, however.

Two grandparents, both his father's parents, had died within the year. Lenny's father had taken these losses very hard. He had missed a great deal of work and was in danger of losing his job.

The outings that Lenny and his father used to take ended. Lenny missed this time together with his father tremendously.

COMMENT. From a strictly neurologic standpoint, not much was required. Neither his clinical course nor his neurologic examination suggested we were dealing with a brain tumor.

His major problem appeared to be his depression. It was clearly tied in with his father's depression and what contributed to that. I recommended psychiatric involvement for both and several months later all the parties involved were better.

You may be nervous about seeing a psychiatrist. But you've helped your child get over that hurdle. So you can do it, too.

Do it. It should pay off for you, your child, and your entire family.

□

PUTTING YOUR OWN EXPERIENCE TO WORK

The psychiatrist or psychologist is obviously a key person in your child's treatment. But there are things you have learned from your own emotional experience that can be very helpful to your child.

This applies whether your child is experiencing major depression now or has recovered but is experiencing a return of some depressive symptoms.

Don't overlook your own potential contributions to treatment!

Dealing with "Everyday Depression"

How do you deal with "everyday depression"? The first thing you should do is realize that you're experiencing some depressive symptoms.

A bit of fatigue. Difficulty getting organized. Feeling sleepy even when you couldn't possibly be tired. Being on the verge of tears for no good reason.

Your child could be experiencing just these kinds of symptoms. He or she should identify these as signals of depression.

Getting Angry at Yourself

If you don't recognize that you're a bit depressed, you may try to "power through it."

You mistake your energyless state as a sign of weakness. You flog yourself with caffeine to try to get yourself going. (Your teenager may try this with amphetamines, cocaine, or other drugs—another clue to the presence of an underlying depression.)

You get angry at yourself for not accomplishing more. (That's something that perfectionistic teenagers, who are among the most vulnerable for suicide, may feel as well as part of their depression.) As a result, you feel worse than ever.

Taking It Easy

If you do recognize what's going on, you let yourself respond to your body's slow-down signals.

You cut back a little. You don't expect quite so much of yourself for a few days. Even a week or two. You do the important things. At least you get the important things ready to tackle.

You don't get down on yourself for operating at less than peak efficiency! Your child shouldn't either.

Having a structure and plan for your day does help. Sitting around stewing in your juices—depressive juices—can get very depressing.

The Depressive Spiral

That can get you into a depressive spiral. The worse you feel, the less you do. The less you do, the worse you feel. And so on. This truly is a vicious cycle.

One way to break it is to mobilize yourself. (Your depressed child may need a push—one step beyond support—something which must be delivered with exquisite care to avoid outright rejection.)

So you get up. Get out. Set a goal for the day. Go to the library and pick out a few books that catch your interest. Call a friend and get together for lunch or a movie. You keep yourself active.

That's a principle your child can understand. It'll make him or her feel better.

□

POSITIVE FEEDBACK

When your daughter has done something which she has enjoyed and which has made her feel better, point that out to her. Reinforce that step in the right direction.

Parent: "Jean, what movie did you see tonight.?"

Jean: "Oh, the latest James Bond."

Parent: "How was it?"

Jean: "Okay. Actually, it was good. It made me laugh for a change."

Parent: "I'm glad you enjoyed it. Have anything on tap for the weekend?"

☐

EXERCISE CAN HELP

Many people find that exercise helps their everyday depression.

Regular aerobic exercise appears to change the chemistry of the brain. It can raise your level of endorphins, naturally occurring brain chemicals that can improve your mood.

Exercise takes you away from the refrigerator and burns up calories. It tends to speed up weight loss and slimming. Looking better can be a helpful step along the path to feeling better.

You may already be using some of these measures to deal with depressive symptoms you experience from time to time. Your son or daughter can apply these same ideas if he or she has symptoms of depression.

☐

A TIMETABLE FOR PROGRESS

As you embark upon treatment for your child, you should ask the therapist for benchmarks to measure improvement.

Bear in mind that prediction is extremely difficult—and earlier predictions may need to be revised. Do try, however, to get an idea of how many weeks and months you should expect to wait before there's an improvement in mood and behavior, a return to a more normal level of activity.

□

REASONS FOR LACK OF PROGRESS

There are several reasons that treatment may not be working.

The therapist and child may simply not hit it off satisfactorily. In that situation, clarify whether that's the problem, and try again—with the same or a different therapist.

Important issues may remain untouched. The child may not yet be willing to share highly personal secrets with his or her therapist.

Sexually abused children may not even be aware of what is causing their depression. It may take several sessions— much doll play combined with astute guesswork by the therapist—before the deeply hidden secret becomes available for discussion.

A key family member may be missing from therapy sessions. Both parents should take part (not necessarily at the same time), even if they're divorced. It is nearly always of significance to know why a particular family member is not participating.

Now that we've looked at psychotherapy, the next chapter will deal with medication and its possible role in treating depression in childhood and adolescence.

The Role
of Medication

W hat is the role of medication in the treatment of depression in childhood and adolescence?

Before I answer this question, let me state my personal bias. Then I'll tell you what I think as a professional who may recommend or prescribe drugs.

□

PERSONAL ORIENTATION

My personal orientation is that I'm not a drug-taking person. I do take medication when it's prescribed by my physician. Fortunately, that has been infrequently. I take aspirin several times per year for garden-variety aches and pains.

I'm even careful about caffeine, a drug that many (if not most) people in this country take daily.

I stopped drinking caffeine-containing beverages eight years ago. Since then I have found that I pace myself better through the day, with less intense ups and downs. I'm more responsive to my body's signals and take a break when I need to.

I accidentally guzzled down two cups of caffeine-containing coffee last year. It obviously didn't kill me. I slept it off, in fact. But I prefer to remain caffeine-free.

□

MY PERSONAL POSITION

I'm not a drug-giving parent, unless it's strictly and clearly necessary and prescribed by the children's pediatrician.

An exception is a little bit of fever medicine, which can go a long way toward making a child with a miserable flu syndrome more comfortable.

I feel that children shouldn't run off to the medicine cabinet whenever something's wrong. They shouldn't think of drugs as the first solution, and certainly not as the only solution, to ordinary medical problems.

□

AS A PHYSICIAN

I do prescribe drugs as a physician, but very thoughtfully and only after carefully weighing the risks against the benefits for each child. I often do this thinking out loud with the family present. At appropriate steps in the process, I invite their comments and suggestions.

In many clinical situations, it's not clear whether to use medication.

For example, should a three-year-old girl who has had two fever convulsions be treated with phenobarbital for prevention of seizures? A reasonable argument can be made on both sides of the issue.

In reaching a recommendation as to drug treatment, I try to reflect reasonable differences of opinion. I might conclude the discussion of pros and cons with the following: "I feel about 75-25 on the side of medication."

This is not medical decision-making by committee. I feel this approach prevents unnecessary shopping around for opinions the family understands and agrees with. It gives them, including the child or adolescent, a greater sense of participation in decision-making. That can only enhance enlightened participation in treatment.

□

ATTENTION DEFICIT DISORDER

I've learned some important lessons from children with attention deficit disorder—the old hyperactive child syndrome.

As most people know, this is a disorder characterized by excessive activity, short attention span, and impulsivity—the tendency to act on the spur of the moment, without thinking even for a split second.

This problem can interfere profoundly with all aspects of a child's life. That's why it's called a "disorder."

Such children often do poorly in school, even if they have a high IQ. They don't have any close friends because they're bossy and get into fights so easily. Their siblings can't stand them.

What's especially sad to say is that very often their parents can't stand them either!

They've had school evaluation, psychological testing, behavior therapy—and it's still a disaster.

□

RITALIN

At some point or other—frequently in my office—the question of medication is raised. The drug at issue is generally methylphenidate—Ritalin—a first cousin of dextroamphetamine (Dexedrine).

Some people may be inappropriately gung-ho to use drugs. Others are inappropriately hesitant.

For starters, treatment is not merely a matter of medication or not. There are many nonpharmacologic measures that can, and should, be used to help the child with attentional disorder. These include smaller classrooms, a self-contained setting, sitting close to the teacher, and individualized instruction in areas of academic difficulty.

In a rush to medication, some of these measures may get left behind.

Some parents hesitate to have their child take drugs because "we don't want our son on 'speed'." Ritalin used in a therapeutic manner, however, in proper dosage is not mood-altering or addictive. The target symptom is attention. And the supervised, thoughtful use of this drug can improve the child's quality of life, and that of his or her family, in a major way.

□

NOT A LAST RESORT

Largely through my experience with the use of Ritalin, I have come to feel strongly that, given the right set of circumstances, the use of medication in childhood and adolescence should not be considered only as a treatment of last resort.

I've never been among the first to recommend a drug that's just come out. It generally has to have been used in children for several years. It must have established a record of safety and efficacy before I'll write a prescription for it for a child.

□

QUALITY OF LIFE

Some medications are called upon in life-or-death situations. Examples of this are antibiotics (such as ampicillin and chloramphenicol) for meningitis and insulin for diabetes.

The situation is different when it comes to disorders of mood and behavior in childhood and adolescence such as attention deficit disorder and depression. This is not usually a matter of life or death. Under these circumstances, I feel that medication is best used when employed to improve the child's quality of life.

□

RONALD

A social worker brought her fourteen-year-old son to see me. "From the time he started school, it's been a struggle for him," she said.

"He tries hard. In fact, he works much harder than my other children ever did. Yet he does poorly and hates school with a passion.

"He comes home and throws his books down. That is, if he's even remembered to bring them home. He's cranky for the rest of the day. Everyone in the family tries to stay out of his way.

"I hate to see him suffer like that. He's a smart kid, a good kid. We've had him tested. But no one can seem to find out what the problem is."

COMMENT. The problem was he had an attention deficit disorder *without* hyperactivity. He was never a "squeaky wheel" calling attention to his struggles.

Not knowing things should be any different, he labored quietly over the years. He had trouble catching the instructions for his assignments, finishing his work in class, and completing tests on time. His best efforts yielded only mediocre grades.

Ronald was becoming increasingly discouraged with his situation.

I started him on Ritalin. It has had a markedly beneficial effect upon his academic life and has made an overall improvement in his well-being.

He has become much better able to complete his classwork in a timely and accurate manner. "He actually enjoys school," his mother said, with a smile. Ronald feels much better about himself and is looking forward to college.

□

PARALLELS WITH DEPRESSION

The treatment of depression shares many parallels with that of attention deficit disorder. Both problems can have a profound and pervasive impact upon all spheres of activity.

Both problems generally affect the entire family, not just the individual child. Hence, the scope of therapy must often be widened to include the family.

With depression as with attention deficit disorder, I do not feel medication should be kept as a measure of last resort. It should be used thoughtfully, for specific reasons, to enhance the child's quality of life.

□

WENDY

Wendy was ten years old when her mother brought her to see me. "She's been miserable on and off for the past three months," her mother said.

"She's cranky. Complains about everything," noted her mother. "Nothing pleases her."

Wendy was quicker to tears and much less active than usual. "She'd rather stay in her room and read or sleep than go bowling with her friends," her mother said.

This crankiness actually went back much further than three months. Her mother felt it began in kindergarten.

"Her nursery school teachers used to call her Sunshine because of her sparkling personality. The next year, she was different. Spacey. Not all there."

She pointed to a subdued picture of her five-year-old daughter and said with emotion: "It's never been sunshine since."

When I examined Wendy, I found her to be an articulate, intelligent girl who did not look at all depressed.

I asked her about these "off" and "on" periods. She acknowledged them with a shrug. Then, while I spoke further with her parents alone, she drew pictures of herself both ways.

Without Energy or Enthusiasm

"I can't sit up an inch," says the stick figure she drew (Fig. 1). It lay back in bed without energy or enthusiasm for anything.

The depressed figure in this drawing contrasts sharply with what she drew to represent what she feels like when she is well (Fig. 2).

"Yes!" replies the full-bodied person responding to the question "Are you finished?" She is sitting upright, leaning forward, ready to tackle another task.

In-Between Mood

It turned out that Wendy spent only around 5 percent of the time in her "off" phase. But her parents indicated that no more than 20 percent of the time—less than a week per month—was she entirely well!

Most of the time she was neither floridly depressed—like the stick figure—nor entirely well.

She was in between. A bit on the cranky side. Tired all the time. Hard to get involved in family activities. Not a pleasure to be around.

Psychiatric Consultation

I asked a psychiatrist to see Wendy in consultation. She met with her and her parents twice. She agreed that there was an

Fig. 1. This is a picture ten-year-old Wendy drew of herself to show what she felt like when she was depressed, what she called being "off."

Fig. 2. This is how Wendy drew herself when she felt well, or "on."

occasional problem with depression, with some lingering irritability.

She wasn't able to identify any particular stresses—such as marital problems, a death in the family, or an impending move—that might be contributing to changes in mood and behavior. She didn't feel that psychotherapy was needed.

A Difficult Decision

What was the next step? I was not then, nor am I now, enthusiastic about medication. I prefer to avoid medication whenever possible.

Wendy's situation, however, was not a good one. True, she didn't spend much time in the depths. But she wasn't up to par most of the time, either.

She spent most of her time in between the two moods. She made it to school, but she didn't enjoy it once she got there. Not even art, which used to be one of her favorite subjects. There was, in fact, an overall lack of joy in her life.

She was withdrawn, irritable, unhappy—and not getting better.

Recognizing the depressive symptoms Wendy continued to have—albeit not enough to constitute a major depression—I recommended a several-month trial of antidepressant medication: imipramine.

What's Happened Since

Imipramine has appeared to help. Her grades improved. Her scores on nationally standardized tests went up sharply between the fifth and sixth grades. Her mood improved. She was a more willing participant in family activities.

She was pleased with the effect of imipramine. But six months later, without her mother's knowledge, she started to skip doses here and there. She felt it was making her drowsy.

After several weeks, her mother recognized a change and called me. "Wendy's cranky again," she said. "She's back to screaming at her brothers for no reason at all."

Once her mother more closely supervised Wendy's taking the medicine, things got back on track.

COMMENT. After looking at Wendy's pictures and reading her story, there can be little or no doubt that depression can affect children.

Her depression, at least elements of it, could be traced back to kindergarten, when she was five years old.

In her case, there didn't seem to be specific events that caused her depression. It was just there—sometimes more, sometimes less.

An Organic Flavor

The only background information of note was an uncle said to have a manic-depressive disorder. This family history plus Wendy's pattern of depressive symptoms gave the whole situation a very organic, biochemical flavor.

That's one of the reasons I wound up recommending medication.

Let me reemphasize that medication was pursued here not as a last resort, nor because this was a desperate situation. It was pursued because Wendy spent so very much of her time miserable. She was living her life at less than half throttle. Without energy, without enthusiasm, without improvement.

What Helped?

How can you know for sure if it was imipramine that was responsible for Wendy's improvement? Maybe M & M's would have done just as well. Maybe it was just coincidence.

In an individual case, you often don't know for sure. In Wendy's case, her mood and behavior worsened appreciably—as her mother perceived and Wendy acknowledged herself—when she stopped taking her medicine regularly.

When she took the imipramine as prescribed once again, her mood and behavior got back on track.

☐

DRUG ON TRIAL

To know for sure, you'd have to set up a special test—a placebo-controlled, double-blind trial.

"Placebo-controlled" means that you compare the drug in question—in this instance, imipramine—with an inactive substitute, a placebo. The placebo can be a harmless starch pill made up to look and taste exactly like imipramine.

"Double-blind" means that neither patient nor doctor knows which is the test drug (imipramine) or the substitute (placebo). Only the pharmacist making up the pills knows, and she's not telling until the trial's over.

Carrying out this trial would require several months. Let's use, for example, a twenty-four-week period broken into four six-week segments. During two of these segments, the child would receive imipramine, during the other two the look-alike pills.

Rating Depressive Symptoms

During the trial period, parents, doctors, and the child herself would rate symptoms of depression (as well as side effects of medication).

Each person would be asked to identify which weeks she took imipramine and which weeks placebo. At the end of the twenty-four-week period, the code would be cracked. Then, it could be determined if imipramine was more effective than the placebo.

Sometimes two different dosage levels of the test drug are employed. I've done that with Ritalin and found it very helpful in determining the best dosage to use.

□

MORE THAN MEDICATION

Medication appears to have helped Wendy. It has not been the only thing pursued, however.

Other parts of the treatment plan have helped, too. For example, it had been upsetting and additionally depressing when missed homework assignments mounted up. So a plan was worked out that Wendy's mother would be notified by the teacher any week that she failed to turn in two assignments in a given subject.

□

WHOM TO TREAT

I don't feel that every child with major depression should be treated with antidepressant medication.

I do feel, however, that every child with depression should be involved in some form of regular psychotherapy. And, if over a reasonable period of time—say, several weeks to a couple of months—the situation is worse (or at least no better), then a trial of medication should be considered.

Particularly when the depression has an "organic flavor" to it, suggesting biochemical disorder, I feel that using antidepressant medication may be well justified, a matter of "fighting fire with fire."

If you think drug treatment should be considered for your child, seek consultation with a psychiatrist experienced in psychopharmacology. That's the study of drugs that influence mood, thought, and behavior through their actions upon the brain.

☐

THE DOWNSIDE TO DRUG TREATMENT

The upside to use of antidepressant medication is that it can contribute significantly to improved mood and behavior. Is there a downside?

There are always negative aspects of any medication—side effects, toxicity with overdosage, and cost, among others.

With imipramine and related members of the tricyclic family (including desipramine), side effects are often present to a minor degree. Only rarely do they require stopping the drug.

A person on imipramine may experience dryness of the mouth and some dizziness upon standing up.

Dry mouth can be dealt with by drinking a lot of water—not soda or juice—or chewing gum (sugar-free to help avoid cavities). Some people suck candy, and destroy their teeth in the process.

Preventing Dizziness

Dizziness can be prevented or minimized by sitting or standing up gradually.

"Don't shoot out of bed like a rocket," I tell my patients. "Sit up, take a deep breath, and stretch. Then, stand up.

"If you feel dizzy, lie down on your side for a minute or so to let the blood get to your head more easily. You can also pump your legs a few times before you get up to prevent dizziness."

Drowsiness

Antidepressant medication may make a person drowsy. This can be a positive effect if your child has had difficulty getting to sleep.

To minimize daytime sleepiness, most or all of the medication is taken at bedtime.

Some persons taking tricyclics will find that their appetite increases and that they have a tremor or shakiness to their hands. These side effects can be annoying but do not usually necessitate discontinuing of the drug.

□

STARTING MEDICATION

Medication is started at a low dosage. It is then increased every three or four days so long as there are no major problems with side effects.

The amount a person goes up to is based on body weight. The range is usually 1½ to 2 milligrams of imipramine (or desipramine) for every pound of weight.

Prior to starting treatment with a tricyclic compound, an electrocardiogram (EKG) is obtained. The reason for this test is that imipramine and desipramine can alter the heart rate and rhythm. In case any irregularities are found later, it's useful to have a baseline EKG available for comparison.

Some doctors recommend an electroencephalogram (EEG), a brain wave study, before antidepressant therapy is begun because of concern that tricyclic compounds might cause seizures.

As a neurologist who deals with seizures very frequently and who has treated quite a few persons with tricyclics, I'm not impressed with the need for the EEG in this situation.

□

OVERDOSE AND SUICIDE PRECAUTIONS

The depressed patient and his or her parents should know the side effects of medication before it is begun.

They should also know that imipramine or desipramine taken in overdosage, as in a suicide attempt, is highly toxic and may be fatal.

That's one reason some have recommended that antidepressant medication be deferred for depressed children and adolescents until they have gotten past the immediate period after a serious suicide attempt.

Syrup of Ipecac

I suggest that, as a preventive measure, syrup of ipecac be kept in the home of all families in which a member is on antidepressant medication. Syrup of ipecac is used to induce vomiting. It thus vigorously and effectively empties the stomach to prevent further absorption.

Syrup of ipecac should not be given to someone who is drowsy. In that situation, there is increased danger of breathing in vomited material. That can be extremely irritating to the lungs and, ultimately, dangerous to the brain.

Before giving your child syrup of ipecac, contact your doctor, hospital emergency room, or poison control center.

Limit Amount of Medication

Another precaution is to limit the amount of medication dispensed at one time. For starters, I would suggest no more than a one-week supply or 1,000 mg, whichever is less.

Others at Risk for Poisoning

Keep in mind that it's not just the depressed child who is at risk for overdosage.

Other family members, particularly younger ones, are vulnerable. They may want to imitate an older brother or sister taking medication. They may be depressed, too, and feel they can get better in a hurry if they take a whole bunch of pills.

Imipramine can be dispensed in so-called blister packs. Each pill is individually wrapped within sheets of ten. This form of packaging can make it difficult for younger children to ingest more than a few at a time.

Restrict Access

Medication should not be left available to any but a restricted few household members. Whether the depressed child takes his or her medication from the bottle should be discussed with your child's therapist. My recommendation is that, in general, parents give medication to their child.

It's a good idea to watch the medicine being taken. Some children may be unable or unwilling to swallow the pills. They push the pill into their gum pouch, tilt their head back, drink some water, and later spit the pill out.

Danger!

Some children will save up the pills and take them all at once. This can have extremely serious, even fatal, consequences.

My introduction to the toxicity of tricyclic compounds taken in overdosage came during my pediatric internship. It's had a strong and lasting effect on me.

□

DONNA

Donna was one of five sisters, all of whom wet their beds. A specialist placed the four oldest girls on imipramine, which can be used in treating bedwetting as well as depression.

The youngest girl, five years old, knew her sisters were getting pills for bedwetting. She wanted to stop, too. So Donna took matters into her own hands and ingested most of a bottle of imipramine tablets.

She spent the next week in the intensive care unit with an irregular heart beat that was extraordinarily difficult to treat. (She also had a problem with urinary retention, but that wasn't particularly life-threatening.)

She recovered fully, and more effective measures were put into place to prevent further mishaps.

COMMENT. Donna's experience, which fortunately had a favorable outcome, underscores the necessity of keeping imipramine—or any other potentially toxic medication— out of a child's reach.

Imipramine was a dirty word in my vocabulary for several years. I do use it and recommend it now when I think it's necessary. But carefully.

□

IMPORTANCE OF PATIENCE

Families and children should be aware that it generally takes three to six weeks on antidepressant medication before improvement becomes apparent. So they need to be patient.

They should also know that if things don't work out well on one medication, they shouldn't lose hope. It's not the last arrow in the quiver—there is another medication that will work.

Some people won't benefit from imipramine but will respond to amytriptyline. Or vice versa. Others will do best on a combination, for example, taking both imipramine and lithium.

□

PRECIPITATING A MANIC EPISODE

Tricyclic medication can bring about a manic episode. Think of it this way: imipramine can bring the mood of a depressed person toward normal. But sometimes it appears to overshoot its mark, driving the mood beyond normal. As a result, a person has symptoms of a manic episode. These may include irritability, talkativeness, and diminished need for sleep.

□

OTHER DRUGS

Lithium may play a role in your child's treatment. It doesn't lift a person from his or her depressed mood. But it appears to stabilize the balancing system that influences or determines mood. In so doing, it can prevent the recurrence of a mood disorder.

Some children do not benefit from lithium. Or it may not be suitable because of side effects such as skin rash or stomach upset.

In that situation, carbamazepine (Tegretol) may be used.

It's been effective in some adults with periodic mood disorders and is being tried in selected children and adolescents.

Other drugs may be used along with antidepressants in the depressed child.

When depression is associated with symptoms of psychosis (such as delusions or hallucinations), chlorpromazine (Thorazine), thioridazine (Mellaril), or haloperidol (Haldol) may be called upon.

These drugs may be useful as well with extremely agitated or violent behavior.

□

DURATION OF TREATMENT

How long should a person be treated?

There is no clear answer. I recommend a period of no less than four months once a normal mood has been restored.

If this four-month period ends in the middle of your child's school year, you may wish to wait until summer vacation to stop it. That's generally done by reducing the dose gradually, over a six-to-eight-week period.

□

WHEN MEDICATION DOES NOT WORK

A common cause of treatment "failure" with medication is simply not waiting long enough for the drug to take effect. It may require four to six weeks, or even longer.

Sometimes the medication chosen is simply not effective. Or it is not used in high enough dosage. Measuring the level of antidepressant drug in the blood can offer guidelines as to optimal dosage.

Noncompliance—not taking the medication as prescribed—is a major cause of treatment failure. Refusing to take medication may reflect an adolescent's discomfort at feeling different from his or her peers.

It may also be part of denying there's a problem at all.

□

ENHANCING COMPLIANCE

To enhance compliance, an important principle is to make sure the child understands why he or she is being asked to take medication.

Doctor: "Jimmy, what is that medicine you're taking, anyway?"

Jimmy: "I don't know. I can't say it right."

Doctor: "It's called imipramine. Do you know why you're taking it?"

Jimmy: "Has something to do with how I feel. Always tired."

Doctor: "That's right. And being tired has something to do with being depressed. How has the medicine been so far?"

Jimmy: "I don't like it."

Doctor: "Why is that?"

Jimmy: "My mouth's too dry."

Doctor: "A lot of children are bothered by that. Here's something you can try that often works for them. Try sucking on a sugar-free mint every now and then. And drink a lot of water.

Jimmy: "Okay, I'll give it a try."

Making the effort to learn what's bugging the child can build rapport and lead to improved compliance.

Increased Awareness

One way the doctor can improve compliance is to increase awareness by asking the child (and parents) to keep a written record of when medication is taken. This should be brought to the doctor's office at the time of follow-up visits.

I make the assumption that everybody misses a dose or two of medication every now and then. That gets me easily into the issue of noncompliance. I simply say: "What do you do when you miss taking your medicine?" It's then easy to add: "How often would you say you take your medication— nearly all the time, most of the time, or just occasionally?"

If it's only occasionally, I then ask directly what the problem is. It may be dry mouth, tremor, or feeling different. Once I know, I can address the problem and, I hope, gain increased compliance.

If the side effect is truly intolerable, then I'm likely to switch to another drug. Making this change based on input from the child, I've strengthened my alliance with the patient and increased the likelihood of successful treatment.

□

PRINCIPLES OF TREATMENT

The child *must* know that there is a name for what he or she is suffering from. It's "depression."

The child *must* know that it's a treatable problem and that it will not go on forever. Getting better, however, will require—for most—participation in psychotherapy and— for some—medication.

It will also require patience. The problem won't go away overnight.

When suicide complicates depression, special measures—including hospitalization—may be required. These and other issues will be discussed in the next chapter.

8

Suicide: Causes and Prevention

"How could you do this to us?" "Couldn't you have told us how bad you felt?"

These are statements made by parents after they learned their eighteen-year-old son had intentionally driven his car into a tree at sixty miles an hour in an attempt to kill himself.

He failed. But did he really fail? What was the purpose of his action? Could it have been prevented? Will he try again? What should his parents do now?

These are but a few of the questions that came out of this incident. Since he survived, many of them should be answerable.

When a suicide attempt results in death, many of the most important questions can never be answered—most important, "Why?"

This chapter is devoted to suicide, a subject closely linked with depression. We'll be looking into what causes it and what can be done to prevent it, based upon my clinical experience and, more importantly, upon some of the excellent work that has been published in the last few years. Several of these studies are listed in the references section (Appendix D) at the end of the book.

This chapter cannot deal comprehensively with all aspects of this complicated and important problem. What I have intended is to address the questions above, among others, and provide practical information to parents of depressed children and adolescents who may be suicidal.

□

WHAT IS SUICIDE?

The simplest definition of suicide is "to take one's own life." I think we would all agree that an adult who buys a gun, loads it with ammunition, writes a note, and shoots himself fatally in the head has committed suicide.

The situation is less clear, however, when we deal with younger persons and with attempts that have less likelihood for a fatal outcome.

What about the seven-year-old boy angered by his mother who walks across a busy street without looking? Is that a suicide attempt?

What about the seventeen-year-old girl who takes ten aspirin and five Valium tablets? That's far below a lethal dose. Is that a suicide attempt?

I would say yes to both questions. But we shouldn't get hung up on the "Is it?" or "Isn't it?" aspect of the situation. Clearly there is an element of real or potential self-harm in each situation.

That must be addressed. An effort must be made in each situation to understand what the child intended and why. In so doing, a treatment plan can be made to prevent further attempts and to relieve the distress that prompted that kind of action.

□

DEGREES OF SERIOUSNESS

All suicide attempts should be taken seriously—very seriously. Even the ingestion of a few pills. Some suicide attempts, though, are decidedly more serious than others. A bullet is usually much more lethal than a pill.

Some suicide attempts are obvious as such. A rope around the neck. Jumping from a tall building.

Others may not be so clear. Teenagers overcome by carbon monoxide while parked in a car with the engine running on a cold night. Falling down a flight of stairs after drinking alcohol.

Some incidents will be correctly recognized as suicidal only through the alertness and intuition of a parent, nurse, pediatrician, or mental health professional. When the teenager is not talking, a little bit of educated guesswork combined with direct questioning can be most rewarding.

☐

EDWARD

Edward, an eighteen-year-old boy with a history of blackouts, destroyed his parents' car in a collision with a tree. He broke his leg but sustained only minor head injuries, not even a concussion.

It was assumed he'd had one of his blackout spells. That's what the police were told at the scene. At the hospital, a different story emerged. He was interviewed with his parents out of the room.

Doctor: "Edward, how have you been feeling lately?"

Edward: "Pretty rotten."

Doctor: "Rotten? What do you mean?"

Edward: "My grandfather used to live with us. Ever since he died, I've felt terrible. Like I haven't gotten over it."

Doctor: "When did he die?"

Edward: "Around two years ago."

Doctor: "It hit you kind of hard, didn't it?"

Edward: "Yeah. It hit everyone hard because it happened so fast. One minute he was well. The next minute he had a stroke and was gone."

Doctor: "That was two years ago. What's happened since then?"

Edward: "I don't know. I guess I just didn't get over it."

Learning of this background of depression, the doctor pursued a line of questioning directed to understanding exactly what happened that led up to the accident.

Doctor: "Edward, tell me what happened earlier today."

Edward: "Well, I was coming home from work, and I just lost control of the car. That's the last thing I remember until the ambulance."

Doctor: "Did you stop off anywhere on your way home?"

Edward: "Yeah, I did."

Doctor: "Was that an errand? Or did you see somebody?

Edward: "I stopped to see my girlfriend."

Doctor: "Your girlfriend?"

Edward: "Yeah. Well, at least she used to be my girlfriend."

Doctor: "You broke up recently?"

Edward: "Yes."

Doctor: "And what was the purpose of the visit?"

Edward: "Just to say hello. Really, to try to get back together."

Doctor: "How did that turn out?"

Edward: "It didn't."

Doctor: "What do you mean?"

Edward: "She refused to see me."

Doctor: "What did you. . . "

At that point Edward interrupted. Calmly and quietly, he said: "That was not an accident. I tried to kill myself."

This was not Edward's first thought of suicide, it turned out. He had hinted to his parents and friends that he was depressed. No one realized just how down he was.

Not even his psychologist. Therapy was in its early stages, since his previous therapist had moved to a different city. He was not yet comfortable with his new therapist. Not yet willing to tell her about thoughts he'd been having of taking pills or crashing his car.

Inpatient Evaluation

Edward was hospitalized on an inpatient psychiatry unit for four weeks. During that time, he met nearly every day with a psychiatrist. He participated in family meetings with a social worker, his parents, and his siblings.

He came to understand more fully the feelings that led to his suicidal act and the background of depression that set the stage.

He took part in group meetings with others on the psychiatric unit. They discussed previous problems, difficulties on the ward, and issues pertaining to discharge from the hospital.

He was discharged (on antidepressant medication) to live with his parents as before. He returned to his full-time job and participated in weekly individual and family therapy.

He continued to meet with the psychiatrist he knew from the hospital, whom he liked and trusted.

COMMENT. Some people feel very guilty and are intensely angry at themselves. Such people could be described as "an accident waiting to happen."

Only it wouldn't be exactly an accident. With their strong sense of guilt, such persons may have a strong need to be punished. As a result, they may engage in risk-taking behavior. They drive too fast; they pass in dangerous, or borderline, situations.

Their behavior has a double-edged payoff. Assuming they survive the risky situation, they get the thrill (and diversion) of the activity plus the satisfaction of having gotten away with something.

If they get injured, they get the punishment they—at some level—were seeking.

Edward's suicide attempt, which anyone would have to agree was a serious one, did not seem to be prompted by guilt. Rather, it seemed to be a combination of anger at being rejected by his girlfriend and persistent depression linked with the death of his grandfather.

Edward was extraordinarily lucky to have (a) survived and (b) survived without apparent brain injury. It is entirely possible—in fact, I think it will prove to be true here—that the suicide attempt will ultimately exert a positive influence upon this young man's life.

That is not to say it will be easy for Edward and his parents. The depression that fueled the suicide attempt will not go away promptly. Indeed, the thought of suicide has entered his mind several times since discharge from the hospital.

"But keeping busy and meeting with my psychiatrist," he said, "has kept me from doing anything to harm myself."

In this case, the boy's mother almost immediately raised the possibility of intentional injury. On the evening of admission, she took the physician aside and asked: "Do you think maybe it wasn't an accident?"

By asking that question, she highlighted the possibility of intentional injury. Thus, she made it less likely that her son would be sent home from the emergency room merely with a tetanus shot and stitches in his scalp.

By contrast, a relatively minor drug overdose can often be managed on an outpatient basis. I fervently hope, though, that the ingestion of a few pills—unlikely to cause great injury itself—is recognized for what it is: the potential prelude to a preventable death.

□

SERIOUS INTENT

Several characteristics have been identified that suggest particularly serious suicidal intent.[1] They are as follows:

The attempt is:

---

[1] See Appendix D, References, Hawton 1986.

1. carried out in isolation
2. timed so that intervention is unlikely
3. carried out in a way that discovery is avoided
4. done with preparations made in anticipation of death
5. carried out with notification of others beforehand
6. pursued with extensive premeditation
7. accompanied by a written suicide note
8. unaccompanied by alerting of others after the attempt

These descriptions are reflected in comments made about a young man who killed himself:

"People knew he was depressed," a woman recalled. "But they didn't pick up on his visiting friends. He hadn't done that for a long time.

"He was touching base with people not so much to say hello as to say good-bye.

"He gave away some of his prized possessions. Like his fishing rod. I think he wanted to make sure it had a good home after he was gone."

□

WHAT COMES BEFORE?

What clues could people have picked up on? His behavior was not what you'd call bizarre. But it was, for him, unusual. If someone had understood the meaning of that behavior, his death might have been prevented.

Studies of children who have committed suicide have noted circumstances that are likely to precede suicide. One of these is when an adolescent anticipates his parent being told about significant misbehavior—a criminal act or, in some instances, academic failure.

Physical and social isolation during the several days prior to committing suicide was also typical. One of the clues was school absence the day of the suicide. The child often stays home alone while his or her parents are off at work.

□

WHY DO YOUNG PEOPLE COMMIT SUICIDE?

Many, perhaps most, children and adolescents who kill themselves are depressed. Others may be psychotic, responding to delusion and hallucinations.

Reasons for suicide include the following:[2]

1. to get relief from a terrible state of mind
2. to escape for a while from an impossible situation
3. to make people understand how desperate they were feeling
4. to make people sorry for the way they had treated them
5. to frighten people or otherwise get back at them
6. to try to get a particular person to change his or her mind
7. to show how much they love someone
8. to find out whether someone really loves them
9. to seek help from someone
10. to be with a loved one who has died

Feelings at the time of a suicide attempt may include anger, loneliness, worry about the future, failure, or shame. It is common for sadness to be lacking entirely!

□

DRUGS AND SUICIDE

Adolescence is a time of experimentation. One of the things

---

[2] See Appendix D, References, Hawton 1986.

adolescents experiment with, unfortunately, is drugs. Drugs and suicide can be linked in several ways.

Drugs, particularly depressants like alcohol and barbiturates, may be used to blunt painful emotions such as depression and anxiety.

Stimulants such as amphetamines and cocaine may be used to counteract directly feelings of depression. After the "high" is over, however, there is generally a "down" phase that often has the look and emotional feel of depression.

That highly unpleasant down state, regardless of its cause, exerts a powerful push toward obtaining and using more drugs. That sets up a self-perpetuating cycle of physiologic and psychologic dependence.

Since such drugs can impair judgment, it makes it easier for an overdose to have a fatal outcome. That can make the line between intention and outcome unclear.

Was a sixteen-year-old girl trying to kill herself when she took an overdose of Valium? Or was she just trying to escape for a few hours when she had a few drinks and misjudged the combined effects of alcohol and Valium?

The bottom line is that, intentional or not, this overdose— any overdose—was harmful and self-inflicted. Thus, it fits well within the spectrum of suicidal behavior.

Failure to appreciate the seriousness of any kind of self-injurious behavior—obvious or not—can lead to a missed opportunity for treatment and, at times, to death.

Other Drug Effects

Rather than blunt emotional pain, some drugs may accentuate a person's suffering or allow her to feel it more acutely. Suicide then provides a way out, a way to stop the pain.

Some drugs may cause delusions. These are false beliefs that are held fixedly, which can strongly influence behavior.

Delusions may be of a paranoid nature—accusatory or persecutory. They may bring about agitated flight from imagined dangers that lead in their panic to death.

Drugs may also release suicidal impulses previously held in check. Under the loosening effects of lower doses of alcohol, a depressed teenager who's had thoughts of killing himself is at increased risk of impulsively killing himself.

□

AGE AND SUICIDE

Does a child really understand enough about death to know what he or she is doing? Is suicide in the adult sense really applicable to children?

I think a lot of ink has been spilled on this issue without much benefit to anyone. Does it really matter what the child intends? The behavior is (or could be) dangerous.

You must recognize that and get your child to safety and a trained professional. Then the issues of cause and intention can be sorted out.

Parents of preteens shouldn't take too much reassurance from the small chance of suicide at that age. Yes, it's true that the likelihood of suicide increases during adolescence. But suicidal behavior has been recognized as early as the preschool years (ages three to five)!

□

"COPY CAT" SUICIDES

That there can be an element of imitation in a young person's suicide, as some people have suspected, has been borne out in recent studies looking at the impact of suicide in television movies.

In a study within the greater New York area, it was found that suicide attempts increased during the two weeks after four fictional films on television dealt with adolescent suicide.

It is ironic and tragic that the apparent intent of these programs—to enlighten and to prevent suicide—appears to have had the opposite effect. (This study did not determine if, in fact, some suicides were prevented.)

As a consequence of this and other studies, it has been recommended that news and dramatic programs on television take special care in presenting stories of suicide. Particularly when the person who has died is a celebrity, the media should not allow the glamour of the star to extend to the act of suicide itself.

□

PARENTAL ISSUES

One of the most gripping questions parents ask their suicidal child—and themselves—is simply "Why?"

Parents of a suicidal child often feel an extraordinary degree of guilt and failure. "If we were doing such a great job," they ask, "how could this possibly have happened?"

"What will others think?" is another concern. Suicide smacks of "craziness." And the family is likely to be extremely uncomfortable about how they will face their neighbors.

Limiting the inevitable spread of the news about their child can be such an important issue that a family chooses to pursue psychiatric care outside their immediate community.

These are issues involving parents that need to be addressed promptly. This can be done at the same time as the child is receiving acute psychiatric help.

□

IS SUICIDE CRAZY?

Is suicide "crazy"? Most of the time, I don't think so. I think it can be understood in very simple terms.

I view suicide, in most instances, as an attempt to gain relief from intolerable feelings. These feelings don't have to stem from special circumstances such as death or divorce. They can arise from some "garden variety" causes, like sibling rivalry.

□

LEON

I saw Leon because of headaches when he was fourteen years old. In speaking with me about this problem, he told me there was something that had been bothering him for a while, since he was nine.

"I was taking a bath and I had a funny feeling," he said. "My whole body got tight and my ears kind of buzzed.

"I stuck my head under the water and thought, 'What would it be like if I breathed in?'

"That made me feel worse. A little scared," he went on. "But I breathed a little water into my nose anyway. I don't know why.

"That ended it, though. I haven't done anything else like that, and I never told anyone about this before."

COMMENT. Studies of unselected groups of high school students have found that up to 20 percent have actually done something to harm themselves.

So when it comes to thoughts—and even actions—of self-harm, we're dealing with a common event.

Where does this come from? After all, as human beings we're programmed for survival, aren't we?

In Leon's case, my brief exploration of his distressing experience from years earlier suggested it stemmed from sibling rivalry. He had a younger sister he adored. He also hated her. And he didn't know what to do about these terrifying angry feelings.

I suspect that his toying with suicide—though it was not viewed in quite that way—was a way of dealing with intense anger and guilt he experienced as a result of that anger.

It's too bad he didn't discuss these feelings with an adult at that time. It might well have spared him much distress.

Since his current headaches appeared to be stress-related, and because I suspected there were other important issues he might wish to discuss, I recommended he meet with a psychiatrist for consultation.

Both in childhood and adolescence, as in adulthood, emotional suffering can feel so great that it seems no longer bearable.

On the other hand, if the pain has eased a bit, the child may despair of ever feeling completely well, or can't bear the thought of going back down into the depths of depression again.

Hopelessness appears to be a key element in many suicides. That should provide an important clue to approaching the suicidal child or adolescent.

☐

AN EFFECT OF SHELTERING?

It has been said that children in our society have been sheltered from so much that when they do experience hard times, they're inexperienced and overwhelmed.

Tuning in to television "tragedies" that resolve neatly within thirty to sixty minutes hardly prepares children for emotionally trying times in their own, real lives.

Their parents may not have prepared them, either. So the children get desperate. They panic. They want to end their pain and suffering by ending their lives.

□

SUICIDE AND PSYCHOSIS

Suicide may occur with psychotic behavior, associated with delusions or hallucinations. For example, a child might respond to voices that tell him to jump into the path of a car.

The mental health professional does consider psychosis as a possibility in evaluating your child and would let you know if it were present.

□

TREATMENT

Treatment of the child or adolescent who has attempted suicide has several important parts. Two of the most important are observation and communication.

The child must be under continuous observation to prevent further attempts at self-harm. This generally involves hospitalization in a setting where such monitoring can be assured. Optimally, such a facility is experienced in dealing with suicide in young people.

The child must have the opportunity to communicate about his or her concerns with qualified mental health professionals. The staff should also work closely with the family to understand what caused the suicide attempt and, particularly, to prevent its recurrence.

☐

"WILL SHE TRY AGAIN?"

Will your child attempt suicide again? There is no certain answer.

Studies have shown that 20 percent to 50 percent of children who attempt suicide once are likely to repeat an attempt.

Suicide remains a possibility. But when your child is given the benefits of professional help and improved communication, you should have increased confidence that he or she will make a healthier choice when encountering emotional difficulties in the future.

☐

PREVENTIVE MEASURES

Parents can take measures that will lessen the chance for suicide. I would recommend the following steps to the parents of any depressed child, not just of those children who are, or have been, suicidal.

• Firearms should be removed from the home. Locking them up is not adequate. Locks can be sawed off, latches removed. Get the guns out of the house!

• Pills no longer required should be thrown away. Those that are required should be kept in secure, out-of-the-way places.

• Antidepressant medication—potentially lethal in overdosage—should be dispensed to the child by a parent. At least in the initial phases of treatment, no more than a week's supply of pills should be kept in the house. Individually wrapped pills in blister packs should be obtained, if available.

• Make sure that pills, if prescribed, are actually taken. Pills can be stuck between cheek and gum, spit out later in private, and saved for a life-threatening overdose.

Issues of Trust

These measures I've just described deal with issues of trust—a critical area pertaining to many aspects of suicide. It would be valuable to discuss these preventive measures with your child's psychiatrist. You may also wish to bring them up at a family meeting.

Syrup of Ipecac

Syrup of ipecac should be kept in your medicine cabinet. If an overdose of medication has occurred, or you suspect it has, call your family doctor, your child's therapist, the emergency room, or the poison center to discuss whether to induce vomiting with ipecac and bring your child to a medical facility.

Ipecac is highly effective in ridding the stomach of unwanted contents before further absorption has taken place. You shouldn't give syrup of ipecac to a drowsy or sleeping person, however, because a diminished state of alertness increases the risk of breathing in vomited material.

Other Preventive Considerations

Going off to college can be academically and socially stressful. If those stresses have contributed to a suicide attempt, the adolescent may do better to live at home (subject to closer parental supervision and guidance), attend school as a day student, and continue with regular psychotherapy.

When attempted suicide has occurred as a consequence of sexual abuse, the child must be assured of a protected environment. This may involve living with relatives or foster parents. Hospitalization may be required.

□

HOPE—THE ESSENTIAL INGREDIENT

Children who have attempted suicide must learn that intolerable feelings often pass with time, if they can only hold on.

These children must also learn that people are available who care about them and who can help them through terrible times.

That person can be a friend, family member, pediatrician, psychiatrist, minister, rabbi, or other caring person.

The main point is not to give up hope.

Having one or more persons to turn to, to reach out to, in times of stress is a crucial element in the prevention of further suicide attempts.

To put it in another way, communication with others is a powerful human instrument in building a positive future.

Now, that we've considered suicide in childhood and adolescence, let's look at organic aspects of depression.

9

The Organic Basis of Depression

Parents are often surprised—and relieved—to learn that the depression their child is suffering from has an organic basis.

What does it mean—"organic basis"? Does that apply to all kinds of depression? Why is that a relief to many?

This chapter is devoted to answering these questions. Briefly, "organic basis" means that depression—the symptom or the disorder, regardless of its cause—is rooted fundamentally in a person's chemical makeup.

Knowing that, parents of a depressed child may feel less guilty. They may feel less responsible for causing the depression by something they did, or failed to do.

I'm not saying that parents may not play an important role in causing the depression of their child. They often do, and they should accept that responsibility.

What I am saying is that many parents are spared unnecessary and sometimes crippling guilt when they become more aware of certain organic, or biological, aspects of their child's depression.

□

EVIDENCE FOR A BIOLOGICAL BASIS

What is there that suggests a biological basis to depression?

Take a step away from depression for a moment. Look at something from your everyday life—sleep.

Have you ever felt a compelling, almost overwhelming urge to sleep? An urge you could fight off for a while, but which ultimately took over? The result was inevitable—you slept.

We've all had that experience, I think. It's as if someone slipped a drug into our evening Ovaltine.

Depression, too, can have that same chemical, drugged flavor. A pervasive, behavior-altering influence that, unfortunately, you can't sleep off (although you might try).

This chemical flavor to depression is illustrated by a teenager I looked after who had two episodes of profound depression that came "out of the blue."

□

DEREK

Derek's father brought his fourteen-year-old son to see me because of a change in his behavior over the preceding two weeks. "When we're in the family room watching TV," he told me over the telephone, "Derek's staring at the wall."

The first thought that ran through my mind was "Uh-oh. This looks like a brain tumor or a degenerative disorder." I didn't have to ask many questions to know I needed to see him soon.

In meeting with Derek and his father, I learned that everything about him had slowed down over those few weeks. He walked, talked, thought, ate, and moved more slowly. His participation in sports fell off markedly, and he was starting to miss school.

He wasn't sad, weepy, or irritable. He was just there.

Sitting before me, Derek was a healthy-appearing, virtually immobile young man. He didn't move around in his seat even a little. His face showed no expression. He initiated no conversation.

When I asked him why he was there to see me, he looked at me, paused, and said slowly, with the appearance of great effort, a single word: "Changes."

He was the picture of marked depression. He made me feel sad. But I could not convince myself *he* felt sad, irritable, angry, anxious, or otherwise discontent. As far as I could determine, he experienced nothing with regard to mood.

Given this profound change in behavior, I could readily appreciate why his parents and his psychiatrist referred him to me for consultation.

His neurologic examination was entirely normal. I carried out a full battery of tests, including a CAT scan of his head, electroencephalogram (brain wave test), thyroid hormone levels, and measurement of serum calcium. All were normal.

(That does not mean that Derek and others like him are not suffering primarily from an organic, biochemical disorder. To me, it means just that we don't yet have the answer. We must keep looking.)

Over the next week, Derek thawed out a bit. His mother noted one good sign. He started acting a little "bratty." Within two weeks, he was back to his usual self.

When I saw him for follow-up examination a month later, I was nearly bowled over by the difference. He conversed freely. He gestured. He was animated (though not manic, or "hyper"). He smiled.

I asked him if he remembered the episode. "Yes," he said. "How did it start?" I inquired. "I was feeling fine," he recalled. "Then a heaviness came over me. It was like a metal spring that passed from one arm to the other through my chest."

I explored with him and his father whether any experiences, especially losses, had occurred that might have triggered this episode. I came up with nothing, as had his psychiatrist. No one in his family had a background of depression.

Three months later, the depressive episode recurred. It lasted two weeks as before, again without any apparent precipitant and without sadness. Since that time, he has been entirely well for at least five years to date.

COMMENT. I was forcibly struck by the overwhelming alien quality to this young man's profound behavioral disturbance. It was as if his mood and behavior were chemically altered for several weeks by an outside force.

He is one of several children and adolescents I have followed over the past decade who have episodic disorders of behavior and mood. Some day we'll be able to test the blood or urine of these children and know what's going on inside them.

Right now, though, we don't have all, or even many, of the answers. The state of the art in testing for depression is not at the needed point yet. What we can say, in essence, is that there appears to be something organic going on when depression occurs.

Needless to say, Derek's parents had little to feel guilty about.

□

FORMULA FOR DEPRESSION

Why does one person become depressed while another person in a similar situation does not?

I look at this difference as a reflection of the differences in chemical makeup between people.

I believe that this chemical makeup is determined largely by genetics, what a person has inherited from parents. This view is suggested by family studies that show how depression runs extensively through some families and not others.

If your body chemistry is "loaded" towards depression, it may take relatively little—by way of minor physical illness or emotional upset—to trigger a depressive episode.

If, on the other hand, your body chemistry is not set up that way, it may take a major stress—emotional or physical—to set off the chemical events that we recognize as depression.

In other words,

Genetic Susceptibility + Life Experience = Depression.

☐

GETTING THE ANSWERS

Which specific chemicals may be involved in depression has been suggested by the side effects caused by the drug reserpine.

Reserpine is a medicine used for treating high blood pressure (hypertension). It works because it interferes with the action of naturally occurring chemicals that maintain or elevate the blood pressure.

The problem is that these chemicals also maintain normal mood. In lowering the blood pressure, reserpine can cause the mood to plunge, too, creating severe and long-lasting depression.

☐

THE "FIGHT OR FLIGHT" CHEMICAL

These naturally occurring substances are called catecholamines. One of them is epinephrine, also known as adrenaline. That's the "fight or flight" chemical released into the bloodstream at times of emergency.

It causes your heart to beat more rapidly. It increases attention. It dilates your pupils. It gets you ready for action. It's a "survival" substance, getting you ready to fight—or flee for your life.

You may recognize these effects as symptoms of anxiety. Indeed, persons who have an anxiety disorder behave as if adrenaline is released at the wrong times or in excessive amount.

Adrenaline is not called into play just in crisis situations. It's involved, too, in everyday maintenance of alertness and mood.

Adrenaline and other catecholamines are made inside nerve cells. These chemicals don't float around haphazardly. They are collected into tiny packets ready for action.

When the nerve cell received a signal—an electrical impulse originating in the brain or another part of the central nervous system—these packets are discharged from the cell. Adrenaline is then available to exert its effects.

☐

A MESSAGE NOT DELIVERED

What would happen if a particular step of this process did not work properly? Let's look at reserpine, which can actually cause depression. It's been found that this drug interferes with normal packaging of adrenaline.

Thus, when the message comes down for adrenaline to be released from the cell, it can't be done. As a result, adrenaline can't get to its destination to carry out its mission.

Putting it in other terms, the movement of information (in electrical and chemical form) from one place in the nervous system to another would be blocked, made sluggish. In fact, sluggish behavior in a depressed person appears to result from just this kind of difficulty—an insufficiency of usable adrenaline or other catecholamine.

Turning the Switch Off

Adrenaline and related chemicals are normally "switched off" in several ways. They can be broken down by other substances, called enzymes. They can be taken up again into the original nerve cell to await further instructions for discharge.

Antidepressant medications appear to work by interfering

with either or both of these mechanisms of inactivation. That is, they can block the enzymes that break down messenger substances (called neurotransmitters) such as adrenaline. They can interfere with recapture of the chemical by its cell of origin.

As a result there is more adrenaline or other neurotransmitter substance available to exert its effect.

This is an oversimplification, to be sure. Substances other than catecholamines (such as serotonin) appear to play an important role in transmitting messages from one nerve cell to another. Antidepressant medications appear to have other important ways of helping, too.

By sketching out some of these events for you, I have hoped to provide an understandable view of the submicroscopic world where, at some level, the battle against depression is being waged.

□

A CHEMICAL BALANCING ACT

The catecholamine story is but one chapter in the book of depression, however. Mood appears to be the result of a complex chemical balancing act.

Some of this delicate balance of chemicals is being revealed through a new medical subspecialty: psychoneuroendocrinology.

Let me break that word down. *Psycho* refers to mood, thought, and behavior. *Neuro* refers to the brain and other parts of the nervous system. *Endocrinology* refers to the study of chemicals made in one part of the body that have an effect upon other parts of the body.

Psychoneuroendocrinology, then, is the study of chemical substances made by the brain that have an impact upon mood, thought, and behavior.

☐

TESTING

Tests are being developed that show how chemical balance is disrupted in depression. What's particularly exciting is that these tests may prove useful in diagnosing depression.

These tests are primarily used by depression researchers in the 1980s. These researchers are trying to determine whether these tests or others like them might be of use outside the laboratory in the 1990s and beyond.

Several tests appear potentially useful. We are a long way, however, from your being able to go down to the neighborhood pharmacy to pick up a kit for the diagnosis of depression.

Pituitary Gland

Three of the most promising tests involve the pituitary gland. This pea-size structure deep within the brain sits at the physiologic crossroad of a great deal of emotional and behavioral traffic.

I think of the pituitary (along with its upper neighbor, the hypothalamus) as a place where emotion gets converted into observable behavior, and experience gets translated into emotion and learning.

Growth Hormone and Depression

One of the substances made by the pituitary is growth hormone. It obviously has something to do with growth. Not so obviously, it has something to do with depression, too.

To see if a person has a normal amount of growth hormone, special tests are carried out. In one of these, a person takes several tablets of the medicine clonidine.

One of the ordinary uses of clonidine is to treat high blood pressure. The growth hormone test is based upon the ability of clonidine to cause an outpouring of growth hormone from the pituitary into the blood, where the increased amounts of growth hormone can be measured.

At least that's what happens in most normal persons who take clonidine. In children and adults with depression, the usual rise in blood levels of growth hormone may be less likely to occur. So, if a person has lower than normal levels of growth hormone, it may indicate major depression.

Thyroid Gland

Another promising test has pretty much the same basis. This is the TRH test, named after thyrotropin-releasing hormone. TRH is a hormone made by the hypothalamus, a part of the brain that directs the pituitary.

TRH controls the production of thyrotropin, a substance made by the pituitary. Thyrotropin in turn switches on the thyroid gland. (I find this fascinating because of the sloweddown, depressed look of those persons whose thyroid is underactive.)

As with the growth hormone test, depressed persons may show a blunted response on the TRH test. In other words, TRH infusion yields less thyrotropin than expected.

The TRH test used in adults has identified persons with very mild hypothyroidism who require treatment with thyroid hormone (in addition to the standard anti-depressant medication) in order to get better.

The Adrenal Connection

The hypothalamus and pituitary are also importantly connected to the adrenal glands. These paired glands play a major role in our adaptation to many kinds of stress.

Tieing into this hypothalamic-pituitary-adrenal axis is the dexamethasone suppression test (more commonly known as the DST). The DST is based upon the normal variation during the day in blood levels of cortisol, a hormone produced by the adrenal glands.

After years of confusion, I've finally found a way to remember how cortisol levels vary during the day. It's simple—up in the morning, down at night. Just like you and me!

Dexamethasone acts pretty much like cortisol. When you take dexamethasone at night as part of the test, the hypothalamus and pituitary "figure" they don't need to make any more cortisol for a while. So cortisol production is temporarily switched off. It's suppressed.

But when you're depressed and you take the dexamethasone suppression test, your cortisol may not be switched off. There is a failure of cortisol suppression.

What does this abnormality mean? It's not fully clear. What can be said is that the state of balance and mutual regulation involving the hypothalamus, pituitary, and adrenal glands is disturbed.

☐

BLOOD TESTS FOR DEPRESSION?

At this point, these tests are used just about exclusively in research. You cannot rest the diagnosis of depression on abnormal test results alone.

But suppose a teenager met some, but not all, criteria for major depression and had several abnormal neuroendocrine test results? Wouldn't that qualify as major depression?

The scientific answer is no. At least not at the present level of our knowledge. My gut feeling, however, is more along the lines of maybe. Within a few years, given further fruitful investigation, it may turn into yes.

As the usefulness of neuroendocrine testing becomes clarified, other uses suggest themselves. For example, would abnormalities on hormone tests indicate a person is likely to benefit from antidepressant medication?

What is the effect of treatment—psychotherapy, medication, or both—on abnormal test results in depressed persons? Can neuroendocrine testing help determine how long a depressed person should be treated?

This decade will, I expect, answer these and other important questions. Neuroendocrine investigation provides a window to the brain that will undoubtedly yield many more important insights into the chemical basis for, and effects of, depression. Such progress will have extremely valuable implications for treatment.

Now that we've looked at the organic side of depression, it's time to look at what the future will hold for the child or adolescent with depression.

10

The Future of the Depressed Child

What is the outlook for the depressed child? The picture is not clear. Or, to be more accurate, it's still being drawn.

It would be valuable to take a group of depressed children and follow them through adolescence into adulthood. Do they have a recurrence of depression? Do these children develop other problems, such as anxiety disorder or manic episodes?

Such studies are in progress, but only preliminary results are currently available. They suggest that children who have been depressed are at somewhat increased risk of developing a further episode of depression.

It would be interesting to take a group of depressed adults and learn about their backgrounds. Were they depressed as children or adolescents? What was done about it?

□

DIFFERENT OUTCOMES

The available data don't allow us to predict what will happen with an individual child. An episode of major depression can be expected to end. It may not come back for months, years, or at all.

Some children and adolescents who have had periods of depression will have other depressive episodes.

Others will go on to have manic episodes. They will thus be considered to have a manic-depressive, or bipolar, disorder.

My guess is that essentially all children and adolescents who have been depressed will have another experience with depression at some point in their lives.

It may be an "everyday depression," however, and not a major depressive disorder. In either instance, you and your child should be better able to deal with the problem through your efforts and increased awareness.

☐

"NORMAL DEPRESSION" IS OKAY

What's most important is not whether depression will return but what to do if it does.

You shouldn't be passive, accepting depression as something you can't do anything about, preventively or therapeutically. You should be active—action-oriented.

Children have told me they can tell quite clearly what's normal depression and what's not.

"Normal depression goes away when you take a nap," one boy told me. "If I'm tired *all* the time, that's a problem.

Appreciating the difference between depression *the reaction* and depression *the disorder,* you can choose to work out the problem through family and friends on the one hand, or seek professional help on the other.

☐

PREPARED FOR THE FUTURE

With these uncertainties about the future, what should you do now?

You should recognize that there are uncertainties to everyone's life. If depression is going to make a reappearance in your life, at least you will be more prepared to recognize it and deal with it.

You and your child should now know what the symptoms are. They might include sleeping too much, persistent crankiness, feeling on the verge of tears for no good reason.

You're not going to let depressive symptoms like these drag on for weeks or months as you might have before depression was first diagnosed.

You're going to get your son or daughter straightaway to a

professional who is experienced in dealing with mood disorders. If medication is needed, you'll understand why and for how long.

You won't let the depression interfere with your child's life more than absolutely necessary.

□

CURRENT RESEARCH

What can be assured is that there will be major advances in our understanding of depression as it affects persons of all ages. Such an increased understanding should have great impact on the prevention and treatment of depression.

Already there are exciting developments. Some people have been found to experience depression during winter months, periods of diminished sunlight. This *seasonal affective disorder* in some persons responds beneficially to light.

Other researchers are exploring how artificial changes made in sleep patterns can be used to treat depression.

I'm not talking about trying to sleep it off. That doesn't work with anything but relatively minor depressions. Evidence in adults, however, suggests that certain kinds of sleep deprivation can have beneficial effects.

Natural History of Depression

Some of the most important information isn't being gathered in the laboratory. It's being obtained in the field.

It's the result of teams of researchers following people over years and seeing what happens in their lives. Some of these people have never been depressed. Others did experience depression during childhood or adolescence.

Does the depression come back? What treatments work

best? Does something new—such as manic behavior or anxiety—enter the picture? How does depression interfere with their lives? Do they have difficulty finishing school, getting married, raising a family, or holding a job equal to their abilities?

This kind of information should go a long way toward addressing many important questions that parents of depressed children have.

Depressed Brains?

Research in neurology is being devoted to the question of whether the brains of depressed people are different.

Some evidence suggests that depression reflects disturbance more of the right side of the brain than of the left. What this means in terms of cause or treatment remains to be clarified.

Other studies involve the brains of persons who have died from suicide. Some research has shown biochemical differences between the brains of suicide victims and those of persons who died of other causes.

The New Biology

With depression in some of its forms being recognized as a familial disorder, its chemical basis is being further elucidated.

From their investigation of families affected by depression, researchers have found a way to identify persons likely to develop a manic-depressive disorder through studying their chromosomes.

Within the next several years, it may be possible to identify more specifically—down to the molecular level—what's wrong with their chromosomes. These studies can be expected to provide a means of genetic counseling and—perhaps someday—even genetic engineering: "fixing" the DNA before a baby is born.

Food-Mood Connection

Another important and fascinating area of research is how nutrients—components of what we eat—influence brain function. In other words, how our food affects how we think, feel, and ultimately act.

Newer and Better Drugs

New drugs are continually being sought in the treatment of depression. Sophisticated research strategies are being used to make sure that these drugs truly do work, not merely through their placebo effect (the power of suggestion and belief).

Newer Tests

The dexamethasone suppression test, thyrotropin-releasing hormone (TRH) test, and growth hormone stimulation test may soon be leaving the laboratory-research setting and entering the realm of clinical utility.

Additional neuroendocrine research will undoubtedly clarify the usefulness of such tests in childhood and adolescence. It should also clarify the basis for the premenstrual syndrome—monthly alterations in mood—that many women experience.

These tests may prove useful not just in diagnosing depression but also in selecting persons who are likeliest to benefit from medication.

□

WHAT ABOUT YOUR OTHER CHILDREN?

You may be concerned about your other children developing depression, too, especially if you or your spouse has a history of depression. Should you be?

I do think you have some reason for concern. Your children are at somewhat increased risk. But there are things you can do to reduce the likelihood of a problem or to minimize a problem should one occur.

Don't tiptoe around your child because you feel he or she is somewhat vulnerable.

If you shield your child from everyday stresses, you may be setting her up for a rude and stressful awakening when she comes up against the world beyond the walls of your home.

□

BUILDING EMOTIONAL HEALTH

Even if no one in your family has a history of depression, there are things you can do that will help develop and maintain your child's emotional health.

First and foremost, children need to be valued. That requires regular and meaningful contact with one or both parents during—and beyond—the first several years of life.

Don't fool yourself by pleading "quality time" to describe what you do. Be honest with yourself. Are you doing more than easing your conscience when you parcel out those few morsels of quality time?

If your children are not near the top of your priority list, your quality time is not going to add up to more than a few bittersweet snapshots once your children have flown through childhood and adolescence.

□

THE OCCASIONAL PARENT

The occasional parent is not one a child is going to turn to in order to disclose worries about death, to express sadness about a dying grandfather, or to drop hints about a teacher's inappropriate touching.

When children are valued, they value themselves. They don't have to fill their lives with empty television watching and recreational eating. Those are futile attempts to achieve stimulation and substance.

The valued child provides stimulation by reading, playing, engaging in sports, carrying out projects, establishing meaningful relationships.

You can help your child through gentle guidance and by setting a good example.

□

DEPRESSED EPISODES VERSUS DEPRESSED LIVES

I've spent a great deal of time discussing episodes of depression in this book. A good many people realize, especially once they've gotten to adulthood, that they were depressed *throughout* their childhood.

Some of those people were simply ignored. Their parents put the food on the table. But that's where the caring stopped.

Others were neglected because their parents had to work so hard to survive or to meet their personal goals. They were physically and emotionally drained. Very little was left for the child.

We all know or have heard about those whom we might call the "fortunate poor." They were given nourishing love and attention despite financial hardships.

These are peculiar economic times. The mien of prosperity and the reality of hardship can occur at the same time. Income rises while quality of life declines. Time slips away as you extend yourself further to keep from falling behind.

□

INVESTING IN YOUR CHILDREN

When it comes to the stock market, some would say the best thing to do is not to participate. We can't afford to do that with our children. We must invest in them. For their future and for the future of our society.

Making our children whole, emotionally healthy beings is one of the most important things we can do for them. There's much we can do as parents to lay the groundwork for their emotional health.

Laying the Groundwork

First, you must recognize that your child is entitled to his or her emotions. That doesn't mean "letting it all hang out" all the time. Children should learn to recognize and identify their feelings. That's something you can help them with:

"Johnny, are you angry?" "Emily, you look sad to me today." "Bill, you're acting cranky. Is something bothering you?"

Emotion as Communication

What you're doing is allowing emotion to be used as a form of communication. You're acknowledging a signal, or a set of signals, your child is expressing—often without words.

With your words and actions, you tie that emotional state to reality. You're making sure your child knows the message is getting through.

You ask: "What's the problem?" "Can I help?" The unspoken message is: "You matter to me. I care."

A lot of life's experiences must be covered alone. Important personal decisions are not made by committee, nor should they be. A parent's support—feelings of empathy and confidence—can launch a child toward his or her own success, whatever that might be.

□

BEING WELL AGAIN

You and your depressed child should realize that you're not alone with this problem. Depression is extraordinarily common. It has affected senators, movie stars, and astronauts.

They've gotten better. And your child should know he or she will, too, given patience and the right kind of help.

Remember, it doesn't so much matter *if* depression occurs. It's what you do about it that counts!

Failure to recognize and deal with depression, as you well know, can be met with emotional suffering, academic underachievement, and even death.

If there is going to be a problem, you will recognize it promptly and get appropriate help for your son or daughter.

I sincerely hope this book has helped you deal with your present situation and that it has given you, your child, and the rest of your family valuable tools for a healthier and happier future.

Manic Syndrome Checklist

The mood of a person with a manic syndrome is abnormally and persistently elevated, expansive, or irritable.

With a manic syndrome, the mood disturbance is sufficiently severe as to interfere significantly in occupational work or other major spheres of activity; or it necessitates hospitalization to prevent harm to self or others.

Three or four of the following symptoms are present in a manic syndrome.

	Present	Absent	
1.	_____	_____	Inflated self-esteem; grandiosity
2.	_____	_____	Decreased need for sleep
3.	_____	_____	Talkative; pressured to keep speaking
4.	_____	_____	Feels that thoughts are racing; flight of ideas
5.	_____	_____	Easily distracted
6.	_____	_____	Agitation; increase in goal-directed activity
7.	_____	_____	Involves self excessively in pleasurable activities with limited regard for consequences

Checklists in Appendixes A-C have been adapted from *Diagnostic and Statistical Manual of Mental Disorders*, Third Edition-Revised, American Psychiatric Association, 1987.

8. _____ _____ Excessive distress (tantrums) in anticipa-
                    tion of parents' leaving home upon even a
                    social occasion
9. _____ _____ Excessive distress when separated from
                    home: desire to return home, call parents

PANIC DISORDER

A panic attack is a discrete period of intense fear, discomfort,
or apprehension that includes at least four of the following
symptoms:

Present Absent

1. _____ _____ Shortness of breath; smothering
                    sensations
2. _____ _____ Dizziness; unsteady feelings; faintness
3. _____ _____ Palpitations; accelerated heart rate
4. _____ _____ Trembling or shaking
5. _____ _____ Sweating
6. _____ _____ Choking
7. _____ _____ Nausea or abdominal distress
8. _____ _____ Depersonalization or derealization
9. _____ _____ Numbness or tingling sensations
10. _____ _____ Flushes (hot flashes) or chills
11. _____ _____ Chest pain or discomfort
12. _____ _____ Fear of dying
13. _____ _____ Fear of going crazy or doing something
                    uncontrolled

Four episodes (essentially unprovoked) must occur within a
four-week period (or at least one panic attack followed by one
month or more of persistent fear of having another attack).

Episodes cannot be accounted for by identifiable organic factors such as drug intoxication (e.g., amphetamines, caffeine) or
metabolic disorder (e.g., hyperthyroidism).

Manic Syndrome Checklist

The mood of a person with a manic syndrome is abnormally and persistently elevated, expansive, or irritable.

With a manic syndrome, the mood disturbance is sufficiently severe as to interfere significantly in occupational work or other major spheres of activity; or it necessitates hospitalization to prevent harm to self or others.

Three or four of the following symptoms are present in a manic syndrome.

	Present	Absent	
1.	_____	_____	Inflated self-esteem; grandiosity
2.	_____	_____	Decreased need for sleep
3.	_____	_____	Talkative; pressured to keep speaking
4.	_____	_____	Feels that thoughts are racing; flight of ideas
5.	_____	_____	Easily distracted
6.	_____	_____	Agitation; increase in goal-directed activity
7.	_____	_____	Involves self excessively in pleasurable activities with limited regard for consequences

Checklists in Appendixes A-C have been adapted from *Diagnostic and Statistical Manual of Mental Disorders*, Third Edition-Revised, American Psychiatric Association, 1987.

Anxiety Disorder Checklists

Anxiety often accompanies depression. Or it can occur by itself as a major problem, a disorder.

to help you recognize what may be significant anxiety, I have included checklists for three anxiety disorders: generalized anxiety disorder, separation anxiety disorder, and panic disorder.

Fill out these checklists and bring them to your doctor for discussion.

GENERALIZED ANXIETY DISORDER

At least six of the following symptoms are generally present during periods of unrealistic or excessive anxiety and worry:

Motor Tension

	Present	Absent	
1.	___	___	Trembling, twitching, or feeling shaky
2.	___	___	Muscle tension, aches, or soreness
3.	___	___	Restlessness
4.	___	___	Easy fatigability

Autonomic Hyperactivity

5.	___	___	Shortness of breath; smothering sensations
6.	___	___	Palpitations; accelerated heart rate
7.	___	___	Sweating or cold, clammy hands
8.	___	___	Dry mouth
9.	___	___	Dizziness or light-headedness

10. _____ _____ Nausea, diarrhea, other abdominal distress
11. _____ _____ Flushes (hot flashes) or chills
12. _____ _____ Frequent urination
13. _____ _____ Trouble swallowing; "lump in the throat"

Vigilance and Scanning

14. _____ _____ Feeling keyed up or on edge
15. _____ _____ Exaggerated startle response
16. _____ _____ Difficulty concentrating; mind "going blank" because of anxiety
17. _____ _____ Trouble falling or staying asleep
18. _____ _____ Irritability

SEPARATION ANXIETY DISORDER

Present *Absent*

1. _____ _____ Excessive worry that harm will befall parents (or other important persons) or that they'll leave and not return
2. _____ _____ Unrealistic, persistent worry that a calamity will separate the child from parents (or other important persons)
3. _____ _____ Persistent reluctance or refusal to go to school in order to stay with parent(s) or other important persons
4. _____ _____ Persistent reluctance to go to sleep without being near parent (or other important person) or to sleep away from home
5. _____ _____ Persistent avoidance of being alone; clinging to, shadowing parents
6. _____ _____ Repeated nightmares involving the theme of separation
7. _____ _____ Physical complaints (such as headache, stomach ache, nausea) on school days or otherwise upon anticipated separation

8. _____ _____ Excessive distress (tantrums) in anticipa-
                     tion of parents' leaving home upon even a
                     social occasion
9. _____ _____ Excessive distress when separated from
                     home: desire to return home, call parents

PANIC DISORDER

A panic attack is a discrete period of intense fear, discomfort,
or apprehension that includes at least four of the following
symptoms:

      Present *Absent*

1. _____ _____ Shortness of breath; smothering
                      sensations
2. _____ _____ Dizziness; unsteady feelings; faintness
3. _____ _____ Palpitations; accelerated heart rate
4. _____ _____ Trembling or shaking
5. _____ _____ Sweating
6. _____ _____ Choking
7. _____ _____ Nausea or abdominal distress
8. _____ _____ Depersonalization or derealization
9. _____ _____ Numbness or tingling sensations
10. _____ _____ Flushes (hot flashes) or chills
11. _____ _____ Chest pain or discomfort
12. _____ _____ Fear of dying
13. _____ _____ Fear of going crazy or doing something
                      uncontrolled

Four episodes (essentially unprovoked) must occur within a
four-week period (or at least one panic attack followed by one
month or more of persistent fear of having another attack).

Episodes cannot be accounted for by identifiable organic factors such as drug intoxication (e.g., amphetamines, caffeine) or
metabolic disorder (e.g., hyperthyroidism).

Attentional Disorder / Hyperactivity Checklist

At least eight of the following symptoms are required to meet the criteria for the presence of attentional disorder with hyperactivity.

	Present	*Absent*	
1.	_____	_____	Restless; fidgets with hands or feet; squirms in seat
2.	_____	_____	Has difficulty keeping to seat
3.	_____	_____	Easily distracted by extraneous stimuli
4.	_____	_____	Has difficulty awaiting turn in games or group activities
5.	_____	_____	Blurts out answers to questions before they have been completed
6.	_____	_____	Has difficulty following through on instructions
7.	_____	_____	Has trouble sustaining attention in play or tasks
8.	_____	_____	Shifts from one activity to another without completing the first
9.	_____	_____	Has difficulty playing quietly
10.	_____	_____	Talks excessively
11.	_____	_____	Often interrupts or intrudes in conversation or play
12.	_____	_____	Does not seem to listen to what is being said

13. _____ _____ Often loses things necessary for school or
home activities

14. _____ _____ Engages in physically dangerous activities without considering possible
consequences

APPENDIX D

References

□

CHAPTER 1: IS YOUR CHILD DEPRESSED? HOW YOU CAN TELL

American Psychiatric Association. *Diagnostic and Statistical Manual of Mental Disorders*. 3rd ed., Washington, D.C.: American Psychiatric Association, 1987. The bible of the mental health professional (though not without controversy), a further step forward in establishing a scientific basis for psychiatric diagnosis, treatment, and prognosis.

Beardslee, W.R.; Klerman, G.L.; Keller, M.B. et al. "But Are They Cases? Validity of DSM-III Major Depression in Children Identified in a Family Study." *American Journal of Psychiatry* 142 (1985): 687-691. Yes, they are—children and adolescents with major depression, a diagnosis which was at times beclouded by drug abuse, attention deficit disorder, and conduct disorder.

Bowlby, J. *Attachment.* New York: Basic Books, 1969. The first of three volumes of *Attachment and Loss,* by the eminent British psychoanalyst John Bowlby.

————. *Separation: Anxiety and Anger.* New York: Basic Books, 1973. Vol. 2 in *Attachment and Loss.*

————. *Loss: Sadness and Depression.* New York: Basic Books, 1980. Vol. 3 in *Attachment and Loss.*

Breslau, N., and Prabucki, K. "Siblings of Disabled Children: Effects of Chronic Stress in the Family." *Archives of General Psychiatry* 44 (1987): 1040-1046. Parents of children who are disabled and demanding of great amounts of care may find their other children quietly—or not so quietly—depressed.

Brumback, R.A., and Staton, R.D. "Learning Disability and Childhood Depression." *American Journal of Orthopsychiatry* 53 (1983): 269-281. Dyslexia can be depressing; there is some neurologic evidence to suggest that right hemisphere dysfunction may be the anatomic basis for depression.

Carlson, G.A., and Cantwell, D.P. "Unmasking Masked Depression in Children and Adolescents." *American Journal of Psychiatry* 137 (1980): 445-49. If you look past symptoms such as bedwetting, school absence, and aggressive behavior in children and seek "adult" symptoms of depression (such as sadness, fatigue, or low self-esteem), you'll very often establish the diagnosis of depression in these children.

Carlson, G.A., and Strober, M. "Manic-Depressive Illness in Early Adolescence: A Study of Clinical and Diagnostic Characteristics in Six Cases." *Journal of the American Academy of Child Psychiatry* 17 (1978): 138-53.

Chambers, W.J. et al. "Psychotic Symptoms in Prepubertal Major Depressive Disorder." *Archives of General Psychia-*

ay reflect chronic physical illness (e.g., asthma)
ive disorder.

P.H. *The Hyperactive Child, Adolescent, and
tention Deficit Disorder through the Lifespan.*
: Oxford University Press, 1987. A longitudinal
ve on a common behavioral disorder that may be
ted by depression.

□

HAPTER 2: GETTING WELL: THE STORY OF THREE CHILDREN

W. et al. "Depression and Panic Attacks: The Signif-
of Overlap as Reflected in Follow-Up and Family
Data." *American Journal of Psychiatry* 145 (1988):

witz, J. "Neurologic Presentations of Panic Disorder
dhood and Adolescence." *Developmental Medicine
hild Neurology* 28 (1986): 617-23. Depression may oc-
the same time as an anxiety disorder, such as a panic
syndrome.

entz, J. *How It Feels When Parents Divorce.* New
Alfred A. Knopf, 1984. Words and photographs of chil-
and adolescents whose parents have divorced.

witz, M.L. "Divorce and the American Teenager." *Pe-
ics* 76 (supplement, 1985): 695-698. More than 12 mil-
children younger than 18 years have divorced parents in
United States; the impact upon children of different ages
the process of being clarified. This paper focuses on
escence.

s, F.N., Jr., and McClure, J.N., Jr. "Lactate Metabolism
nxiety Neurosis." *New England Journal of Medicine
(1967): 1329-1336. Fascinating, important article telling

try 39 (1982): 921-27. About one-third of prepubertal children with major depression reported psychotic symptoms, primarily hallucinations (visual, auditory, and tactile), the pathologic significance of which is unclear.

Chiles, J.A.; Miller, M.L.; and Cox, G.B. "Depression in an Adolescent Delinquent Population." *Archives of General Psychiatry* 37 (1980): 1179-84. Among 120 adolescents (13 to 15 years old), 23 percent met diagnostic criteria for depressive disorder. A family history of depression or alcoholism significantly predicted depression in the adolescent.

Davis, R.E. "Manic-Depressive Variant Syndrome of Childhood: A Preliminary Report." *American Journal of Psychiatry* 136 (1979): 702-706. Although they may appear to be hyperactive, such children seem to have a syndrome different from the usual attention deficit disorder with hyperactivity. In addition to hyperactivity, they have violent temper outbursts, aggressive behavior, and often a family history of manic-depressive disorder.

Fine, P.; McIntire, M.S., and Fain, P.R. "Early Indicators of Self-Destruction in Childhood and Adolescence: A Survey of Pediatricians and Psychiatrists." *Pediatrics* 77 (1986): 557-568.

Gammon, G.D.; John K.; Rothblum, E.D. et al. "Use of a Structured Diagnostic Interview to Identify Bipolar Disorder in Adolescent Inpatients: Frequency and Manifestations of the Disorder." *American Journal of Psychiatry* 140 (1983): 543-47.

Herskowitz, J., and Rosman, N.P. "Depression." In *Pediatrics, Neurology, and Psychiatry—Common Ground.* New York: Macmillan, 1982, pp. 111-38. Describes the organic basis for depression, what looks like depression and isn't (such as a disorder affecting the facial muscles), and what tests the physician should consider in evaluating the depressed child.

Hoier, T. S., and Kerr, M.M. "Extrafamilial Information Sources in the Study of Childhood Depression." *Journal of the American Academy of Child and Adolescent Psychiatry* 27 (1988): 21-33. As with attention deficit disorder, important diagnostic information can be obtained from persons other than the child (or adolescent) and his or her parents. Teachers, peers, and other outside observers can provide valuable information.

Kandel, D.B., and Davies, M. "Epidemiology of Depressive Mood in Adolescents: An Empirical Study." *Archives of General Psychiatry* 39 (1982): 1205-12.

Kashani, J.H.; Holcomb, W.R.; and Orvaschel, H. "Depression and Depressive Symptoms in Preschool Children from the General Population." *American Journal of Psychiatry* 143 (1986): 1138-1143. Provides evidence for existence of major depressive disorder in preschool children (2½ to 7 years; mean age 4) and emphasizes the importance of teachers' reports in identifying depression in this age group. Presents the GRASP questionnaire, developed by Dr. Orvaschel for depression in preschool children.

Kashani, J.H.; McGee, R.O.; Clarkson, S.E. et al. "Depression in a Sample of 9-Year-Old Children." *Archives of General Psychiatry* 40 (1983): 1217-23. Nearly 4 percent of the population were diagnosed as being depressed; behavioral symptoms detected by parents were major indicators of mood disturbance.

Ling, W.; Oftedal, G.; and Weinberg, W. "Depressive Illness in Childhood Presenting as Severe Headache." *American Journal of Diseases in Childhood* 120 (1970): 122-24. Headache and stomach ache are common somatic (physical) complaints that may provide clues to the presence of depression.

Mitchell, J.; McCauley, E [...] "Phenomenology of Depre[...] cents." *Journal of the Amer[...] olescent Psychiatry* 27 (198[...] of 95 children and adolescent[...] ing separation anxiety disord[...]

Poznanski, E.; Mokros, H.B.; [...] Criteria in Childhood Depres[...] *Psychiatry* 142 (1985): 1168-7[...]

Rosenthal, N.E.; Carpenter, C.J[...] Affective Disorder in Children a[...] *Journal of Psychiatry* 143 (19[...] pressive symptoms such as irrit[...] culties, sadness, and sleep change[...] tween 6 and 17 years, all of wh[...] treated with light.

Rutter, M.; Izard, C.E.; Read, P.B[...] *Young People: Developmental an[...] New York: Guilford Press, 1986.

Ryan, N.D.; Puig-Antich, J.; Ambro[...] cal Picture of Major Depression i[...] cents." *Archives of General Psychi[...] Among depressed children from 6 to[...] dren had more physical complaints a[...] adolescents more hypersomnia, wei[...] use. The two groups, however, sha[...] symptomatology.

Spitzer, R.L.; Endicott, J.; and Robins,[...] nostic Criteria. Rationale and Reliabilit[...] *eral Psychiatry* 35 (1978): 773-782.

Weitzman, M. et al. "School Absence: A [...] diatrician." *Pediatrics* 69 (1982): 739-74[...]

absence [...] or depress[...]

Wender, [...] *Adult: A[...] New Yor[...] perspecti[...] complica[...]

Coryell[...] icance [...] Study [...] 293-30[...]

Hersk[...] in Chi[...] and C[...] cur at[...] attac[...]

Krem[...] York:[...] dren [...]

Lebo[...] diat[...] lion [...] the [...] is i[...] ado[...]

Pit[...] in [...] 277[...]

about how lactic acid given intravenously can trigger typical panic attacks in susceptible persons—demonstrating organic, biochemical aspects of an emotional disorder.

Sheehan, D.V. *The Anxiety Disease.* New York: Bantam Books, 1983. Describes normal anxiety versus pathologic anxiety—"the anxiety disease." Details the progression from panic attacks to extensive phobic avoidance (agoraphobia), reviews causes and treatments.

Sheehan, D.V. et al. "Some Biochemical Correlates of Panic Attacks with Agoraphobia and Their Response to a New Treatment." *Journal of Clinical Psychopharmacology* 4 (1984): 66-75.

Van Winter, J.T., and Stickler, G.B. "Panic attack syndrome." *Journal of Pediatrics* 105 (1984): 661-665. Presents a family in which three consecutive generations were involved with the syndrome.

Wallerstein, J.S. "Children of Divorce: Report of a Ten-Year Follow-Up of Early Latency-Age Children." *American Journal of Orthopsychiatry* 57 (1987): 199-207.

□

CHAPTER 3: WHAT TO DO IF YOU THINK YOUR CHILD IS DEPRESSED

Brent, D.A.; Crumrine, P.K.; and Varma, R.R. et al. "Phenobarbital Treatment and Major Depressive Disorder in Children With Epilepsy." *Pediatrics* 80 (1987): 909-917. There is significantly increased incidence of major depression among children treated with phenobarbital versus carbamazepine (Tegretol). An alternative explanation might be that this result stemmed from carbamazepine's well-recognized mood-altering potential effects.

Christen, A.G., and Cooper, K.H. "Strategic Withdrawal from Cigarette Smoking." *CA—A Cancer Journal For Clinicians* 29 (1979): 96-107. An overview of smoking cessation approaches, coauthored by Kenneth Cooper, the "father of aerobics."

Dubovsky, S.L., and Franks, R.D. "Intracellular Calcium Ions in Affective Disorders: A Review and a Hypothesis." *Biological Psychiatry* 18 (1983): 781-97.

Faulstich, M.E. "Psychiatric Aspects of AIDS." *American Journal of Psychiatry* 144 (1987): 551-556. Fear of AIDS can cause anxiety and depression. The disease itself can cause or be associated with mood disturbance as well as psychomotor deterioration that can resemble depression.

Grant, L. Personal communication. Suggestion of the "slouch sign" as described by Dr. Grant, a specialist in adolescent medicine, is gratefully acknowledged.

Herskowitz, J., and Rosman, N.P. "Behavioral Regression" and "Headaches." In *Pediatrics, Neurology and Psychiatry—Common Ground.* New York: Macmillan, 1982, pp. 159-94, 278-316. These are among the categories of physical disease to be considered in the medical evaluation of children who appear depressed.

Herson, G.B., and Johnston, D.A. "Hypothalamic Tumor Presenting as Anorexia Nervosa." *American Journal of Psychiatry* 133 (1976): 580-82. Appetite disturbance, often prominent with depression, may occur as a consequence of direct involvement of the appetite centers of the brain, situated in the hypothalamus.

Jaffe, J.H. "Drug Addiction and Drug Abuse." In *The Pharmacological Basis of Therapeutics.* 7th ed. Edited by Gilman et al. New York: Macmillan, 1985, pp. 532-581. A review of definitions and principles.

Kovacs, M.; Feinberg, T.L.; Crouse-Novak, M.A. et al. "Depressive Disorders in Childhood: I. A Longitudinal Prospective Study of Characteristics and Recovery." *Archives of General Psychiatry* 41 (1984): 229-237.

Ling, M.H.M.; Perry, P.J.; and Tsuang, M.T. "Side Effects of Corticosteroid Therapy: Psychiatric Aspects." *Archives of General Psychiatry* 38 (1981): 471-477.

McLellan, A.T.; Woody, G.E.; and O'Brien, C.P. "Development of Psychiatric Illness in Drug Abusers. Possible Role of Drug Preference." *New England Journal of Medicine* 301 (1979): 1310-14. There is some evidence to suggest that methadone, morphine, and heroin may be used to self-medicate symptoms of anxiety, depression, and paranoia.

Millman, R.B. "Evaluation and Clinical Management of Cocaine Abusers." *Journal of Clinical Psychiatry* 49 (supplement, 1988): 27-33. The stimulation of cocaine may be the abuser's antidote for depression.

Nelson, R.L. "Hypoglycemia: Fact or Fiction?" *Mayo Clinic Proceedings* 60 (1985): 844-850. Discusses the necessity to document hypoglycemia, that is, obtain blood for glucose determination at the time of symptoms to define the correlation, if any.

Petersen, P. "Psychiatric Disorders in Primary Hyperparathyroidism." *Journal of Clinical Endocrinology* 28 (1968): 1491-95. Excessive calcium levels were often associated with lack of energy and affective depression, reversed with removal of the parathyroid tumor that was causing the hypercalcemia.

Pope, H.G. "Drug Abuse and Psychopathology." *New England Journal of Medicine* 301 (1979): 1341-43.

Rodin, G., and Voshart, K. "Depression in the Medically Ill:

An Overview." *American Journal of Psychiatry* 143 (1986): 696-705.

Schottenfeld, R.S., and Cullen, M.R. "Organic Affective Illness Associated with Lead Intoxication." *American Journal of Psychiatry* 141 (1984): 1423-26.

Smith, C.K. et al. "Psychiatric Disturbance in Endocrinologic Disease." *Psychosomatic Medicine* 34 (1972): 69-86. Describes profound changes in mentation with disturbances involving calcium, seroid hormones, glucose, and thyroid hormones.

Whybrow, P.C.; Prange, A.J., Jr.; and Treadway, C.R. "Mental Changes Accompanying Thyroid Gland Dysfunction: A Reappraisal Using Objective Psychological Measurement." *Archives of General Psychiatry* 20 (1969): 48-63. In this study, depression was a common emotional accompaniment to hypothyroidism (thyroid underactivity) in contrast to anxiety and irritability with hyperthyroidism.

□

CHAPTER 4: PREPARING FOR PSYCHIATRIC CONSULTATION

Lewis, M. "Child Psychiatric Consultation in Pediatrics." *Pediatrics* 62 (1978): 359-64.

□

CHAPTER 5: WHAT THE PSYCHIATRIST DOES

Krementz, J. *How It Feels When a Parent Dies.* New York: Alfred A. Knopf, 1983. Statements and photographs of children who have lost a parent through death.

Simmons, J.E. *Psychiatric Examination of Children.* 2nd ed. Philadelphia: Lea and Febiger, 1974.

Freeman, N. "Children's Drawings: Cognitive Aspects." *Journal of Child Psychology and Psychiatry* 17 (1976): 345-50.

□

CHAPTER 6: TREATMENT OF DEPRESSION

Aylward, G.P. "Understanding and Treatment of Childhood Depression." *Journal of Pediatrics* 107 (1985): 1-8. An overview for the pediatrician.

Cantwell, D.P. "Issues in the Management of Childhood Depression." In *Affective Disorders in Childhood and Adolescence. An Update.* Edited by D.P. Cantwell and G.A. Carlson. New York: Spectrum, 1983, pp. 354-362.

Goldstein, S., and Solnit, A.J. *Divorce and Your Child.* New Haven: Yale University Press, 1984.

Hendin, D. "Children and Death." In *Death as a Fact of Life.* New York: W.W. Norton, 1973. Describes how early experience can have a profound impact on later behavior and how the "too good" child may be experiencing an abnormal reaction to the loss through death of a loved one.

Livingston, R. et al. "Family Histories of Depressed and Severely Anxious Children." *American Journal of Psychiatry* 142 (1985): 1497-1499. Emphasizes importance of seeking mood disorder among parents of children and adolescents with anxiety or depressive disorders.

Rosenthal, N.E.; Carpenter, C.J.; and James, S.P. et al. "Seasonal Affective Disorder in Children and Adolescents." *American Journal of Psychiatry* 143 (1986): 356-358. Preliminary study shows several hours per day of bright light can markedly improve depressive symptoms in some children and adolescents.

Shaffer, D. "Depression, Mania and Suicidal Acts." In *Child and Adolescent Psychiatry: Modern Approaches.* 2nd ed. Edited by M. Rutter and L. Hersov. Oxford: Blackwell, 1985, pp. 698-719.

Wegman, M.E. "Annual Summary of Vital Statistics— 1986." *Pediatrics* 80 (1987): 817-827. Cites 1,159,000 divorces in 1986, with just over a million children younger than 18 years affected.

Weissman, M.M.; Gammon, G.D.; John, K. et al. "Children of Depressed Parents: Increased Psychopathology and Early Onset of Major Depression." *Archives of General Psychiatry* 44 (1987): 847-853. Onset of depression tended to be earlier among children of depressed parents (12 to 13 versus 16 to 17 years).

Weller, E.B.; Weller, R.A.; and Fristad, M.A. "Assessment and Treatment of Childhood Depression." In *Major Depressive Disorders in Children.* Edited by E.R. Weller and R.A. Weller. Washington, D.C.: American Psychiatric Press, 1983, pp. 19-35. Underscores value of family therapy in treatment of childhood and adolescent depression.

☐

CHAPTER 7: THE ROLE OF MEDICATION

Ballenger, J.D., and Post, R.M. "Carbamazepine in Manic-Depressive Illness: A New Treatment." *American Journal of Psychiatry* 137 (1980): 782-790. Carbamazepine (Tegretol), used in the treatment of seizure disorders, trigeminal neuralgia, and diabetes insipidus, appears to be beneficial in some persons with manic-depressive illness.

Biederman, J., and Jellinek, M.S. "Psychopharmacology in Children." *New England Journal of Medicine* 310 (1984): 968-972. A brief review of drugs for treatment of depression, anxiety, attention deficit disorder, and psychosis in childhood.

DeLong, G.R. "Lithium Carbonate Treatment of Select Behavior Disorders in Children Suggesting Manic-Depressive Illness." *Journal of Pediatrics* 93 (1978): 689-94.

Garfinkel, B.D.; Wender, P.H.; Sloman, L.; O'Neill, I. "Tricyclic Antidepressant and Methylphenidate Treatment of Attention Deficit Disorder in Children." *Journal of the American Academy of Child Psychiatry* 22 (1983): 343-348. When children with an attention deficit disorder/hyperactivity syndrome have significant mood disturbance, they may do better on an antidepressant (in this study, desipramine) which also has attention-enhancing properties than on methylphenidate, whose predominant effect is on attention.

Glassman, A.H.; Schildkraut, J.J.; Orsulak, P.J. et al. "Tricyclic Antidepressants—Blood Level Measurements and Clinical Outcome: An APA Task Force Report." *American Journal of Psychiatry* 142 (1985): 155-62. Blood level measurements of imipramine, desipramine, and other antidepressant drugs can be of considerable help, and is likely to be used increasingly.

Herskowitz, J. "Children Whose Mothers Have Panic Disorder: A New Category of ADD?" *Neurology* 36 (supplement 1, 1986): 179. Breaks attention deficit disorder into several categories, including those in which depression plays a promi-

nent role and others with significant anxiety. These disturbances in mood may have implications for choice of
medication.

Law, W., III; Petti, T.A.; and Kazdin, A.E. "Withdrawal
Symptoms after Graduated Cessation of Imipramine in Children." *American Journal of Psychiatry* 138 (1981): 647-650.
Children tapered off of imipramine over a 3- to 10-day period (mean 6.4 days) experienced significant withdrawal
symptoms (such as drowsiness, gastrointestinal complaints,
headaches, tearfulness, and insomnia), suggesting that a period of several weeks would be better.

Popper, C. "Child and Adolescent Psychopharmacology."
Chapter 59 in *Psychiatry* (Michels, R. et al., editors). Philadelphia: J.B. Lippincott Co., 1985.

Post, R.M. et al. "Prophylactic Efficacy of Carbamazepine
in Manic-Depressive Illness." *American Journal of Psychiatry* 140 (1983): 1602-1604. Reports that patients with bipolar disorder who benefited from carbamazepine (Tegretol)
were unresponsive to lithium.

Prien, R.F. and Kupfer, D.J. "Continuation Drug Therapy
for Major Depressive Episodes: How Long Should It be
Maintained?" *American Journal of Psychiatry* 143 (1986):
18-23. Study in adults suggests withdrawal of drug therapy
only after the patient has been free of significant symptoms
for sixteen to twenty weeks.

Puig-Antich, J.; Perel, J.M.; Lupatkin, W. et al. "Imipramine
in Prepubertal Major Depressive Disorders." *Archives of
General Psychiatry* 44 (1987): 81-89. This double-blind study
showed beneficial responses both with placebo and imipramine. Among those who responded to imipramine, plasma
levels of imipramine and desipramine (a breakdown prod-
uct) were higher than among nonresponders. Hence, if an

antidepressant drug is used, measurement of plasma levels may be valuable.

Quitkin, F.M. et al. "Duration of Antidepressant Drug Treatment: What Is an Adequate Trial?" *Archives of General Psychiatry* 41 (1984): 238-45. A significant number of adults responded to antidepressant therapy after a six-week trial but not after four weeks, emphasizing the need for patience in treatment with antidepressant medication.

Richardson, J.W., III, and Richelson, E. "Antidepressants: A Clinical Update for Medical Practitioners." *Mayo Clinic Proceedings* 59 (1984): 330-37.

Tosteson, D.C. "Lithium and Mania." *Scientific American* 244 (1981): 164-74. A description of cellular and molecular mechanisms by which lithium is felt to exert its therapeutic effects.

Wehr, T.A., and Goodwin, F.K. "Can Antidepressants Cause Mania and Worsen the Course of Affective Illness?" *American Journal of Psychiatry* 144 (1987): 1403-1411. The answer to this question, based on this study in adults, is probably yes. The available evidence suggests that some persons with bipolar affective disorder (manic-depressive illness) become manic when they are treated with antidepressant medication.

Weinberg, W.A., and Emslie, G. "Attention Deficit Disorder: A Form of Childhood Depression or Other Disorders of Brain." *International Pediatrics* 2 (1987): 135-145.

Weller, E.B.; Weller, R.A.; and Fristad, M.A. "Lithium Dosage Guide for Prepubertal Children: A Preliminary Report." *Journal of the American Academy of Child Psychiatry* 25 (1986): 92-95. Study of 15 prepubertal children (6 to 12 years of age) with very aggressive behavior and mood disturbance, considered to have a form of childhood manic disorder.

Youngerman, J., and Canino, I.A. "Lithium Carbonate Use in Children and Adolescents: A Survey of the Literature." *Archives of General Psychiatry* 35 (1978): 216-24. Review of 190 cases of lithium carbonate use in childhood and adolescence.

□

CHAPTER 8: SUICIDE: CAUSES AND PREVENTION

Arnstein, R.L. "The Place of College Health Services in the Prevention of Suicide and Affective Disorders." In *Suicide and Depression Among Adolescents and Young Adults.* Edited by G. Klerman. Washington, D.C.: American Psychiatric Press, pp. 335-61.

Beck, A.T. et al. "Hopelessness and Eventual Suicide: A 10-Year Prospective Study of Patients Hospitalized With Suicidal Tendencies." *American Journal of Psychiatry* 142 (1985): 559-563. Among hospitalized depressed adult patients, the degree of hopelessness was correlated with the degree of suicidal risk.

Black, D.W.; Winokur, G.; Nasrallah, A. "Suicide in Subtypes of Major Affective Disorder: A Comparison with General Population Suicide Mortality." *Archives of General Psychiatry* 44 (1987): 878-880.

Boyd, J.H. "The Increasing Rate of Suicide by Firearms." *New England Journal of Medicine* 308 (1983): 872-74. While the rate of suicide by all other means has remained the same for the past twenty-five years, the rate of suicide by means of handguns has risen significantly.

Breier, A., and Astrachan, B.M. "Characterization of Schizophrenic Patients Who Commit Suicide." *American Journal of Psychiatry* 141 (1984): 206-209. This study seeks to render more comprehensible what can be a most unpredictable suicide, occurring in a schizophrenic person.

Deykin, E.Y.; Alpert, J.J.; and McNamarra, J.J. "A Pilot Study of the Effect of Exposure to Child Abuse or Neglect on Adolescent Suicidal Behavior." *American Journal of Psychiatry* 142 (1985): 1299-1303. Adolescents with suicidal behavior were three to six times more likely to come from families registered with the state public welfare department for child abuse or neglect than from a group of nonsuicidal adolescents.

Eisenberg, L. "Does Bad News About Suicide Beget Bad News?" *New England Journal of Medicine* 315 (1986): 705-707. Editorial noting the high incidence in deaths (1,700) among American adolescents 15 to 19 years of age and reviewing the "Werther effect," imitative suicides that occurred two centuries ago after publication of Goethe's *The Sorrows of Young Werther.*

Faber, A., and Mazlish, E., *Siblings Without Rivalry.* New York: Norton, 1987. Presents long-standing, intense feelings of anger, rage, and jealousy that siblings must often contend with, and which can be turned against the self in a suicidal manner.

Fishbain, D.A. et al. "Relationship Between Russian Roulette Deaths and Risk-Taking Behavior: A Controlled Study." *American Journal of Psychiatry* 144 (1987): 563-567. This extreme form of risk-taking behavior, often complicated by alcohol or other drug use, may stem from depression. It can be a way to commit suicide or to self-treat mood disorder through the "thrills" involved in defying fate.

Fowler, R.C.; Rich, C.L.; and Young, D. "San Diego Suicide Study: Substance Abuse in Young Cases." *Archives of General Psychiatry* 43 (1986): 962-65. More than 50 percent of young suicide victims abused drugs such as marijuana, alcohol, and cocaine.

Frommer, D.A. et al. "Tricyclic Antidepressant Overdose: A Review." *Journal of the American Medical Association* 257 (1987): 521-26.

Gelenberg, A.J. "Tricyclic Overdoses: Let the Dead Teach the Living." *Biological Therapies in Psychiatry* 8 (1985): 17-18. Describes the use of activated charcoal, a substance which adsorbs the drug in the stomach to prevent its being taken up into the bloodstream.

Gisper, M. et al. "Predictive Factors in Repeated Suicide Attempts by Adolescents." *Hospital and Community Psychiatry* 38 (1987): 390-93. Authors found repeaters to be less successful in school, to display more hostility, to report more dysphoria, and to have undergone more long-term stress.

Gould M.S., and Shaffer, D. "The Impact of Suicide in Television Movies." *New England Journal of Medicine* 315 (1986): 690-94. A study providing evidence of imitation in some teenage suicides.

Greensher, J.; Mofenson, H.C.; and Caraccio, T.R. "Ascendency of the Black Bottle (Activated Charcoal)." *Pediatrics* 80 (1987): 949-951. Activated charcoal may in the near future replace syrup of ipecac as the mainstay of acute poisoning treatment. Check with your pediatrician to learn the latest findings.

Hawton, K. *Suicide and Attempted Suicide Among Children and Adolescents.* Developmental Clinical Psychology and Psychiatry, vol. 5. Beverly Hills: Sage Publications,

1986. A comprehensive book on suicide by a British expert.

Hergenroeder, A.C. et al. "The Pediatrician's Role in Adolescent Suicide." *Pediatric Annals* 15 (1986): 787-98. Describes the pediatrician's unique position to identify adolescents' risk for suicide.

Hodgman, C.H. "Recent Findings in Adolescent Depression and Suicide." *Developmental and Behavioral Pediatrics* 6 (1985): 162-70. Emphasizes the importance of the medical professional asking if the adolescent is depressed or suicidal.

Holden, C. "Youth Suicide: New Research Focuses on a Growing Social Problem." *Science* 233 (1986): 839-841. Reviews the "psychological autopsy" studies of Shafii and Shaffer.

Holinger, P.C. "Violent Deaths as a Leading Cause of Mortality: An Epidemiologic Study of Suicide, Homicide, and Accidents." *American Journal of Psychiatry* 137 (1980): 472-476. Violent deaths (suicide, homicide, and accidents) noted to be the leading cause of death in people aged one to 39 years.

Hudgens, R.W. "Preventing Suicide." *New England Journal of Medicine* 308 (1983): 897-98. An eloquent editorial presenting an overview of measures for prevention of suicide: "Depressed people who kill themselves are not simply upset over life's losses, such as divorce, death of a relative, or unemployment. Rather, they suffer from that usually curable disorder of brain function, a major affective disorder, which has robbed them of the capacity to sustain enthusiasm, energy, and mental efficiency, and has plagued them with an agitated spirit and the often irrational conviction that life is not worth living and never will be."

Klagsbrun, F. *Too Young to Die: Youth and Suicide.* New

York: Simon and Schuster, 1981. Focusing on adolescence, this book keys in on warning signs of impending suicide.

Klerman, G.L., ed. *Suicide and Depression Among Adolescents and Young Adults*. Washington, D.C.: American Psychiatric Press, 1986.

Mack, J.E., and Hickler, H. *Vivienne: The Life and Suicide of an Adolescent Girl*. Boston: Little, Brown, 1981. A remarkable collaborative effort involving a psychoanalyst, a teacher, and the family of a fourteen-year-old girl who killed herself by hanging.

Pfeffer, C.R. *The Suicidal Child*. New York: Guilford, 1986. Takes off from the critical observation that suicide does occur in the preadolescent child, then presents a comprehensive approach to diagnosis and treatment.

Pfeffer, C.R. et al. "Normal Children at Risk for Suicidal Behavior: A Two-Year Follow-Up Study." *Journal of the American Academy of Child and Adolescent Psychiatry* 27 (1988): 34-41. This study followed seventy-five preadolescents (around twelve years of age) without prior psychiatric care for a period of two years. Nearly 18 percent reported suicidal ideas; 1.5 percent made suicidal threats. No child attempted suicide. Based on previous studies, depression and preoccupation with death were considered to be among the factors that would make suicide more likely to occur.

————."Suicidal Behavior in Child Psychiatric Inpatients and Outpatients and in Nonpatients." *American Journal of Psychiatry* 143 (1986): 733-38. Recent and past depression were significantly associated with suicidal behavior.

Phillips, D.P., and Carstensen, L.L. "Clustering of Teenage Suicides After Television News Stories About Suicide." *New England Journal of Medicine* 315 (1986): 685-89. An examination of the relation between suicides and thirty-eight nationally televised news or feature stories about suicide in 1973-79, providing evidence of imitation in teenage suicides.

Rich, C.L.; Young D.; and Fowler, R.C. "San Diego Suicide Study: I. Young vs. Old Subjects." *Archives of General Psychiatry* 43 (1986): 577-82. Notes the significantly increased occurrence of drug abuse among younger suicide victims.

Robbins, D.R., and Alessi, N.E. "Depressive Symptoms and Suicidal Behavior in Adolescents." *American Journal of Psychiatry* 142 (1985): 588-92.

Robins, E. *The Final Months: A Study of the Lives of 134 Persons Who Committed Suicide.* New York: Oxford University Press, 1981. An intensive study of an unselected series of adults who committed suicide in the St. Louis area during a one-year period (1956-1957).

Rosenthal, P.A., and Rosenthal, S. "Suicidal Behavior by Preschool Children." *American Journal of Psychiatry* 141 (1984): 520-525. Study of sixteen suicidal children 2½ to 5 years, noting depressive symptoms and high incidence of parental abuse and/or neglect.

Roy, A. "Family History of Suicide." *Archives of General Psychiatry* 40 (1983): 971-974. Based on a review of records of adult psychiatric inpatients, this study found an increased incidence of depression and suicide attempts in relatives of persons who had committed suicide.

Roy, A., ed. *Suicide.* Baltimore: Williams and Wilkins, 1986.

Ryan, N.D.; Puig-Antich, J.; Ambrosini, P. et al. "The Clinical Picture of Major Depression in Children and Adolescents." *Archives of General Psychiatry* 44 (1987): 854-861. Points to increased suicide risk in adolescents with duration of depressive episode of over two years.

Shaffer, D. "Suicide in Childhood and Early Adolescence."

Journal of Child Psychology and Psychiatry 15 (1974): 275-291. An in-depth analysis of thirty-one children 12 to 14 years of age who committed suicide.

Shaffer, D. "Developmental Factors in Child and Adolescent Suicide." In *Depression in Young People: Clinical and Developmental Perspectives.* Edited by M. Rutter; C.E. Izard; and P.B. Read. New York: Guilford, 1986, pp. 383-96.

Shaffer, D. and Fisher, P. "The Epidemiology of Suicide in Children and Young Adolescents." *Journal of the American Academy of Child Psychiatry* 20 (1981): 545-65.

Shafii, M. et al. "Psychological Autopsy of Completed Suicide in Children and Adolescents." *American Journal of Psychiatry* 142 (1985): 1061-64. A detailed look at twenty children and adolescents (ages 12 to 19), emphasizing that "talkers" (those who speak about committing suicide) often become "doers."

Tavani-Petrone, C. "Psychiatric Emergencies." *Primary Care* 13 (1986): 157-67. A review for the primary care physician, emphasizing that "once a patient is assessed as being suicidal, he or she must not be left alone and should not be sent home."

Tsuang, M.T.; Boor, M.; and Fleming, J.A. "Psychiatric Aspects of Traffic Accidents." *American Journal of Psychiatry* 142 (1985): 538-546. Underscores the well-established link between alcohol use and traffic accidents, but does not describe a definite link between vehicular accidents and suicidal wishes.

Weinberg, W.A., and Emslie, G.J. "Depression and Suicide in Adolescents." *International Pediatrics* 2 (1987): 154-59. Depression from a neurologic as well as a psychiatric standpoint, noting a 13 percent to 18 percent prevalence of depressive symptoms among an unselected high school population.

□

CHAPTER 9: THE ORGANIC BASIS OF DEPRESSION

Baldessarini, R.J. *Biomedical Aspects of Depression and Its Treatment.* Washington, D.C.: American Psychiatric Press, 1983.

Cade, J.F.J. "The Story of Lithium." In *Discoveries in Biological Psychiatry.* Edited by F.J. Ayd, Jr., and B. Blackwell. Philadelphia: Lippincott, 1970, pp. 218-29.

Cooper, J.R.; Bloom, F.E.; and Roth, R.H. "Catecholamine Theory of Affective Disorder." In *The Biochemical Basis of Neuropharmacology.* 5th ed. New York: Oxford University Press, 1986, pp. 304-308.

Dolan, R.J., and Calloway, S.P. "The Human Growth Hormone Response to Clonidine: Relationship to Clinical and Neuroendocrine Profile in Depression." *American Journal of Psychiatry* 143 (1986): 772-74.

Emslie, G.J.; Weinberg, W.A.; Rush, A.J. et al. "Depression and Dexamethasone Suppression Testing in Children and Adolescents." *Journal of Child Neurology* 2 (1987): 31-37.

Ettigi, P.G., and Brown, G.M. "Psychoneuroendocrinology of Affective Disorder: An Overview." *American Journal of Psychiatry* 134 (1977): 493-501.

Geller, B.; Rogol, A.D.; and Knitter, E.F. "Preliminary Data on the Dexamethasone Suppression Test in Children with Major Depressive Disorder." *American Journal of Psychiatry* 140 (1983): 620-22.

Glassman, A.H., and others of the American Psychiatric Association Task Force on Laboratory Tests in Psychiatry. "The Dexamethasone Suppression Test: An Overview of Its

Current Status in Psychiatry." *American Journal of Psychiatry* 144 (1987): 1253-1262. The DST appears to be of limited clinical usefulness in adults. An abnormal result does not predict a beneficial response to antidepressant medication in a person with major depression. A normal result is not an indication for withholding antidepressant medication if otherwise indicated. Continued research on the DST was recommended in view of abnormalities demonstrated in the hypothalamic-pituitary-adrenal axis.

Greden, J.F.; Albala, A.A.; Haskett, R.F. et al. "Normalization of Dexamethasone Suppression Test: A Laboratory Index of Recovery from Endogenous Depression." *Biological Psychiatry* 15 (1980): 449-58.

Ha, H.; Kaplan, S.; and Foley, C. "The Dexamethasone Suppression Test in Adolescent Psychiatric Patients." *American Journal of Psychiatry* 141 (1984): 421-23.

Herskowitz, J., and Rosman, N.P. "Depression." In *Pediatrics, Neurology, and Psychiatry—Common Ground*. New York: Macmillan, 1982, pp. 111-38. Reviews the organic basis for depression, including anatomic and biochemical aspects.

Herskowitz, J., and Turnbull, B.A. "Neuroendocrine Studies of Depression in Adolescent Males." *Neurology* 37 (Supplement 1, 1987): 110. Use of a battery of neuroendocrine tests to try to define abnormalities in adolescents determined to be depressed by DSM-III criteria. Pilot data showed TRH test to differentiate between depressed and nondepressed subjects.

Krishnan, K.R. et al. "Growth Hormone-Releasing Factor Stimulation Test in Depression." *American Journal of Psychiatry* 145 (1988): 90-92. This study takes off from the finding that many depressed persons have a relatively diminished output of growth hormone in response to clonidine. The normal to elevated responses of depressed persons in this study to growth hormone-releasing factor indicate that the problem does not lie with the pituitary, but higher up—presumably at the level of the hypothalamus.

Maas, J.W.; Koslow, S.H.; Davis, J. et al. "Catecholamine Metabolism and Disposition in Healthy and Depressed Subjects." *Archives of General Psychiatry* 44 (1987): 337-44.

Petty, L.K. et al. "The Dexamethasone Suppression Test in Depressed, Dysthymic, and Nondepressed Children." *American Journal of Psychiatry* 142 (1985): 631-33.

Post, R.M., and Ballenger, J.C., eds. *Neurobiology of Mood Disorders.* Frontiers of Clinical Neurosciences, vol. 1. Baltimore: Williams and Wilkins, 1984.

Prange, A.J., Jr., and Utiger, R.D. "What Does Brain Thyrotropin-Releasing Hormone Do?" *New England Journal of Medicine* 305 (1981): 1089-90.

Puig-Antich, J.; Novacenko, H.; Davies, M. et al. "Growth Hormone Secretion in Prepubertal Children with Major Depression: I. Final Report on Response to Insulin-Induced Hypoglycemia During a Depressive Episode." *Archives of General Psychiatry* 41 (1984): 455-460. Study showing blunted response (diminished growth hormone) to insulin-induced hypoglycemia.

Rubin, R.T.; Poland, R.E.; Lesser, I.M. et al. "Neuroendocrine Aspects of Primary Endogenous Depression. I. Cortisol Secretory Dynamics in Patients and Matched Controls." *Archives of General Psychiatry* 44 (1987): 328-36.

Schlesser, M.A.; Winokur, G.; and Sherman, B.M. "Hypothalamic-Pituitary-Adrenal Axis Activity in Depressive Illness: Its Relationship to Classification." *Archives of General Psychiatry* 37 (1980): 737-743.

Siever, L.J., and Davis, K.L. "Overview: Toward a Dysregulation Hypothesis of Depression." *American Journal of Psychiatry* 142 (1985): 1017-31, 1985.

Siever, L.J.; Uhde, T.W.; and Jimerson, D.C. et al. "Plasma Cortisol Responses to Clonidine in Depressed Patients and Controls." *Archives of General Psychiatry* 41 (1984): 63-68.

Slover, R.H. et al. "A Comparison of Clonidine and Standard Provocative Agents of Growth Hormone." *American Journal of Diseases in Childhood* 138 (1984): 314-317. Clonidine is a potent agent for promoting the release into the blood of growth hormone. It does not have the often unpleasant hypoglycemic side effects of insulin used to promote release of growth hormone.

Sternberg, D.E. "Biologic Tests in Psychiatry." *Psychiatric Clinics of North America* 7 (1984): 639-650.

Swann, A.C.; Koslow, S.H.; Katz, M.M. et al. "Lithium Carbonate Treatment of Mania: Cerebrospinal Fluid and Urinary Monoamine Metabolites and Treatment Outcome." *Archives of General Psychiatry* 44 (1987): 345-54.

Targum, S.D., and Capodanno, A.E. "The Dexamethasone Suppression Test in Adolescent Psychiatric Inpatients." *American Journal of Psychiatry* 140 (1983): 589-91.

Weller, E.B.; Weller, R.A.; and Fristad, M.A. et al. "Dexamethsone Suppression Test and Clinical Outcome in Prepubertal Depressed Children." *American Journal of Psychiatry* 143 (1986): 1469-70.

□

CHAPTER 10: THE FUTURE FOR THE DEPRESSED CHILD

Akiskal, H.S.; Downs, J.; Jordan, P. et al. "Affective Disorders in Referred Children and Younger Siblings of Manic-

Depressives. Mode of Onset and Prospective Course." *Archives of General Psychiatry* 42 (1985): 996-1003. Does not define risk of manic-depressive parent having a child with a mood disorder, but does look at the symptoms and progression thereof of referred patients.

Bear, D.M. "Hemispheric Specialization and the Neurology of Emotion." *Archives of Neurology* 40 (1983): 195-202. Describes the right hemisphere as being dominant for many emotional functions.

Beardslee, W.R., and Podorefsky, D. "Resilient Adolescents Whose Parents Have Serious Affective and Other Psychiatric Disorders: Importance of Self-Understanding and Relationships." *American Journal of Psychiatry* 145 (1988): 63-69. Although children whose parents have major depression are at risk themselves for emotional disorder, some (perhaps many) do well. This study of eighteen such persons follows them over two and a half years and explores why they have done well.

Bowlby, J. "Developmental Psychiatry Comes of Age." *American Journal of Psychiatry* 145 (1988): 1-10. The eminent British psychiatrist looks at research that seeks to clarify what determines mental health.

Coccaro, E.F., and Siever, L.J. "Second Generation Antidepressants: A Comparative Review." *Journal of Clinical Pharmacology* 25 (1985): 241-260. A discussion of such agents as trazodone, doxepin, maprotiline, amoxapine, and nomifensine.

Corwin, H.A. Personal communication, The contributions of Dr. Corwin in giving shape and substance to several of the concepts in this chapter are gratefully acknowledged.

Cytryn, L.; McKnew, D.H.; Zahn-Waxler, C. et al. "A Developmental View of Affective Disturbances in the Children of

Affectively Ill Parents." *American Journal of Psychiatry* 141 (1984): 219-222.

Eastwood, M.B.; Whitton, J.L.; Kramer, P.M.; Peter, A.M. "Infradian Rhythms: A Comparison of Affective Disorders and Normal Persons." *Archives of General Psychiatry* 42 (1985): 295-299. A study of infradian rhythms (cyclic patterns occurring over periods greater than 24 hours) in sleep, energy, and mood comparing normal persons with those with affective disorder. It demonstrated that affective symptoms appear to be universal, with normal, physiological differences shading into pathologic variants.

Greiff, B.S., and Munter, P.K. *Tradeoffs: Executive, Family and Organizational Life.* New York: Mentor, 1980.

Hammen, C.; Gordon, D.; Burge, D. et al. "Maternal Affective Disorders, Illness, and Stress: Risk for Children's Psychopathology." *American Journal of Psychiatry* 144 (1987): 736-41. This study compared children whose mothers had affective disorders with those whose mothers had a chronic medical illness or were normal.

Kandel, D.B., and Davies, M. "Adult Sequelae of Adolescent Depressive Symptoms." *Archives of General Psychiatry* 43 (1986): 255-262. A nine-year follow-up study.

Kolata, G. "Manic-Depression Gene Tied to Chromosome 11." *Science* 235 (1987): 1139-40. Based upon a study of Old Order Amish in Lancaster County, Pennsylvania, this research has shown 60 percent to 70 percent of persons who inherit this marker on chromosome 11 develop manic-depressive disorder.

Kovacs, M.; Feinberg, T.L.; Crouse-Novak, M. et al. "Depressive Disorders in Childhood: II. A Longitudinal Study of the Risk for a Subsequent Major Depression." *Archives of General Psychiatry* 41 (1984): 643-49.

Mann, J.J. et al. "Increased Serotonin-2 and Beta-Adrenergic Receptor Binding in the Frontal Cortices of Suicide Victims." *Archives of General Psychiatry* 43 (1986): 954-59. Suggests a rationale for certain antidepressant drugs in the prevention of suicide.

Parry, B.L. et al. "Treatment of a Patient with Seasonal Premenstrual Syndrome." *American Journal of Psychiatry* 144 (1987): 762-66. Bright artificial light reversed severe two-week premenstrual depressions during fall and winter months.

Pray, L.M., and Evans, R., III. *Journey of a Diabetic.* New York: Simon and Schuster, 1983. In this tale of a diabetic, a young man lives with, and ultimately accepts, his chronic condition.

Puig-Antich, J.; Novacenko, H.; Davies, M. et al. "Growth Hormone Secretion in Prepubertal Children with Major Depression. III. Response to Insulin-Induced Hypoglycemia After Recovery from a Depressive Episode and in a Drug-Free State." *Archives of General Psychiatry* 41 (1984): 471-75.

Rosenthal, N.E.; Carpenter, C.J.; James, S.P. et al. "Seasonal Affective Disorder in Children and Adolescents." *American Journal of Psychiatry* 143 (1986): 356-358. Seven children are presented with symptoms of seasonal affective disorder similar to that found in adults. Symptoms included irritability, fatigue, school difficulties, sadness, and sleep changes. Some of these symptoms were reversed by treatment with light.

Rosenthal, N.E., et al. "Antidepressant Effects of Light in Seasonal Affective Disorder." *American Journal of Psychiatry* 142 (1985): 163-170. A study looking primarily at a group of adult women with recurrent fall-winter depressions and spring-summer episodes of hypomania.

Rubinow, D.R., and Roy-Byrne, P. "Premenstrual Syndromes: Overview from a Methodologic Perspective." *American Journal of Psychiatry* 141 (1984): 163-172. A very murky (though important) area, which this article seeks to clarify.

Strober, M., and Carlson, G. "Bipolar Illness in Adolescents With Major Depression: Clinical, Genetic, and Psychopharmacologic Predictors in a Three- to Four-Year Prospective Follow-up Investigation." *Archives of General Psychiatry* 39 (1982): 549-55. Twenty percent of sixty adolescents (13 to 16 years) hospitalized for major depression developed manic-depressive disorder, an outcome made more likely by a family history of bipolar disorder and a hypomanic response to antidepressant medication.

Vogel, G.W. et al. "Improvement of Depression by REM Sleep Deprivation: New Findings and a Theory." *Archives of General Psychiatry* 37 (1980): 247-53. A pilot study of young adults whose depression improved after interruptions during REM (rapid eye movement) sleep, when most dreaming takes place.

Wehr, T.A.; Jacobsen, F.M.; Sack, D.A. et al. "Phototherapy of Seasonal Affective Disorder." *Archives of General Psychiatry* 43 (1986): 870-75.

Weissman, M.M. et al. "Children of Depressed Parents: Increased Psychopathology and Early Onset of Major Depression." *Archives of General Psychiatry* 44 (1987): 847-853.

Wilt, J. *Surviving Fights with Your Brothers and Sisters.* Columbus, Ohio: Weekly Reader Books, 1978. A book for children, giving them the opportunity to read about and discuss issues that may otherwise be difficult to talk about.

——. *Handling Your Ups and Downs.* Columbus, Ohio: Weekly Reader Books, 1979. Helping the child recognize in himself or herself and in others different emotional states.

"Tell It Again"*
—A Song for Children

This is a song I wrote for children. Adults may find that it applies to them as well. The song emphasizes the importance of reaching out and communicating—particularly when it comes to difficult subjects like depression, suicidal thoughts, fear of AIDS, or sexual abuse.

CHORUS
> If you tell and you aren't heard,
> Then—tell it again.
>
> If you tell and nobody listens.
> Tell somebody else.
> It doesn't have to be
> Someone near you,
> You'll find a person out there
> Who is gonna hear you.
>
> If you tell and you aren't heard.
> Then—tell it again.

VERSES
> I went to my mother and I told her
> What's goin' on.
> I went to my mother and told her
> What's wrong.
> She said: "I can see you're upset.

You'll feel better in the morning.
Go to bed."

CHORUS

A couple days later after school,
I stayed late.
I told my teacher I'd something
Important to say.
"It's about what's been happ'nin'
To a friend."
She said: "Sorry—got a meeting
To attend."

CHORUS

I cried myself to sleep that night,
And many more.
I tried to figure out
What life was living for.
I feel bad about
What I've done.
I feel bad 'bout
Telling someone.

CHORUS

I went to a doctor
'Cause my head was killing me.
There was no one else around,
So I told her. I felt free.
She looked me in the eye

And touched my hand. She said:
"I'm glad that you told.
I understand."

CHORUS

---

*Copyright 1986 by Joel Herskowitz. Recorded copies are available on tape cassette through Diskobolos Music, Box 482, South Station, Framingham, MA 01701.

I N D E X